W9-CJG-977

In Defense of the West

American Values Under Siege

Donald J. Devine

UNIVERSITY PRESS OF AMERICA,® INC.

Dallas • Lanham • Boulder • New York • Oxford

University Press of America,® Inc.
4501 Forbes Boulevard
Suite 200
Lanham, Maryland 20706
UPA Acquisitions Department (301) 459-3366

PO Box 317
Oxford
OX2 9RU, UK

Library of Congress Control Number: 2004100976
ISBN 0-7618-2822-2 (clothbound : alk. ppr.)
ISBN 0-7618-2823-0 (paperback : alk. ppr.)

♾™ The paper used in this publication meets the minimum
requirements of American National Standard for Information
Sciences—Permanence of Paper for Printed Library Materials,
ANSI Z39.48-1992

For Josh, Bobby, Billy, John, Matthew,
Jessica, Kathleen, Christopher, Erin, Megan, and Jeffrey

Contents

Foreword

This book is the outgrowth of a series of lectures given by Dr. Devine in our Kirkpatrick Signature Series in Western Vision and American Values at Bellevue University.

As an academic who strongly believes that education has an essential role in shaping and maintaining a just and free society, I have long been interested in a multidisciplinary approach to teaching Western values. I first established such a course at Hillsdale College and brought the concept with me to Bellevue College in 1985. I secured a grant from the Teagle Foundation in New York to establish Bellevue University's undergraduate Signature Series in Western vision and American values as a required course for graduation. A few years later, Berniece and William Grewcock agreed to support an endowed chair for the Series that led to Dr. Devine's affiliation with the program and the university. In light of what has happened in recent years, symbolized so tragically and heroically by the events of September 11, 2001, my long-term goal to ensure that Bellevue University graduates are truly "educated" for a quality life, productive work, and involved citizenship has become even more important for society.

From the beginning, the course was to cover three major topics. First, Western civilization and its values—where students were to explore American culture, its formative events and literature, and its charter documents such as the Declaration of Independence and the Constitution. Second, tradition and change—where students were to study American historic traditions and how societal changes and the interplay between the two have affected society and the individual. Finally, the course was to cover freedom and individual responsibility—where students were to explore the implications and reasoned defenses of freedom in Western history and their responsibilities to ensure a just and productive society.

Dr. Devine took these major elements and, through his own understanding and insights, translated them into the work that is before the reader. As the book was being written, the events of September 11 intervened and focused the book around the threats to Western civilization, including but not limited to that of radical Islam. Terrorism represents a true threat and challenge to our way of life. It is a "counter-civilization" advocated by ruthless, self-appointed zealots. Their goal is to establish and rule a "Counter Utopia," if you will, one that honors deception rather than truth, death rather than life, bondage rather than freedom, one that destroys rather than builds, and one that considers any means acceptable, including mass murder.

In the wake of one of America's worst days, our President and leaders at all levels unified, took the reins, and spoke of justice rather than vengeance and our resolve as a people to stay the course and keep moving ahead. It is the same resolve that Lincoln spoke of at Gettysburg, "that we here highly resolve that these dead shall not have died in vain, that this nation under God shall have a new birth of freedom." I am confident that such resolve exists in abundance in our people.

Freedom must continually be reborn and defended. But our defense of freedom cannot simply be built on anger that fades, for the defense of freedom is never fully secured. We must have a real understanding of the ideas, values, and commitments that underlie our freedom and keep its bright light shining. While Dr. Devine approaches these values in a detached, Socratic, and learned manner, the commitment to those values shines through and makes them even more compellingly attractive because that reasoning so effectively lends its further support to those same values.

The success of the United States is not an accident, and it cannot be preserved by military might alone. A great society arises from great ideas, values, and vision. It also is created during a long process of development and refinement. It is as important to understand that just as a free and prosperous society is not an accident, it is also not the natural state of human affairs. Failure to understand our seminal ideas and values and failure to defend and promote them is at our own peril. At best, universities tend to take our heritage for granted, and at worst, our foundations are systematically attacked. Hopefully, this book and the ideals it represents somewhat redress that imbalance.

Dr. John Muller, President of Bellevue University

Preface

Socrates taught that learning starts with questioning. Evolving as this book did from a dynamic classroom setting, it too relies upon Socratic questioning to draw the reader actively into the ideas of Western civilization. As the learning in the classroom was two-way, with students and fellow professors contributing to its development, so the book that opens here before you likewise seeks an interactive dialogue with the reader. It relies heavily upon raising questions that are only answered gradually as the book develops, both to keep readers engaged and to not quickly dismiss the concerns of those not inclined to support its thesis. That thesis—relatively unique in the academic world today—is that the Western vision and American values are worth questioning or even defending.

The book starts with the September 11 attack and how the values of the terrorists were the important "weapons" causing the destruction, underscoring the need to be aware of all world traditions. The major traditions of the original peoples, of Hinduism, Buddhism, Judaism, Christianity, Islam, conservatism, progressivism, self-reliance, and existentialism are introduced as alternative belief systems, and readers are asked to consider the central values of each. All of these traditions are viewed as coming under stress when they are opened to outside forces. A short history of the Islamic-Christian/West relationship is presented as an example. In the modern world with its instant communication and rapid transportation, all traditions are now questioned, and none can be taken for granted as they once might have been.

New cultural ideas nonetheless have challenged existing ones for a very long time. It is not a new phenomenon. The example of ancient Athens is given, how its extensive commerce brought it into contact with other cultures and led to the questioning of its own traditions. Socrates generalizes this questioning and introduces his view to the world that tradition hides reality and that truth lies behind it. Plato's Republic presents an ideal society that confronts the veiled reality, one designed to achieve justice by "scraping the canvas clean" of the traditional values. This ideal seriously challenges traditional views of the family, government, and society generally. Additional questioning continues through Aristotle, Aquinas, Descartes, and Bacon down to Marx, Nietzsche, Ayer, Darwin, and Freud all the way to postmodernists today. Under this questioning process, values become increasingly challenged as immaterial and unscientific and, finally, mythical and meaningless. Yet, there remains a hesitation, even from the postmodernists, to break from the idea of values completely.

We start with Athens as the most popular candidate for the source of Western values but note that both its great thinkers and the moderns who have commented upon them dispute what was most important about Greece that defined the broader tradition. Alternatively, Jerusalem is investigated as the possible foundation for the Western vision. Then Rome, early Christianity, medieval Christianity, and finally Britain are analyzed as potential sources of the Western vision and American values. We conclude, following the reasoning of many that it was all of these that contributed to what is unique about the West, transferred to America primarily through the writings of the philosopher John Locke.

Next we illustrate how that Western vision was embedded into America's founding documents and institutions, from the Mayflower Compact, the Maryland Act of Toleration, *Poor Richards Almanack*, The Declaration of Independence, the Constitution, the Bill of Rights, and *The Federalist Papers* to the early America described by the French aristocrat Alexis de Tocqueville. American values as then rooted in the Constitution were tested early by slavery and, to a lesser extent at the time, by women's suffrage. Frederick Douglas, Abraham Lincoln, Abigail Adams, and Mary Wollstonecraft criticized major aspects of the original arrangement and changes were proposed for the regime as alternative means to deal justly with these issues. Ralph Waldo Emerson, especially, preached a whole new theory of individual morality, which differed radically from that described by de Tocqueville as the one characteristic of the founding period.

With the old Constitutional regime questioned and torn asunder by actual civil war, all of the old political questions were raised again in America. Alternative views are contrasted with the Declaration of Independence on the matters of community, government, and individual responsibility. These raise the question of whether there is any responsibility to government or community or other individuals. The question of responsibility leads to the idea of character, where Aristotle, Benjamin Franklin, George Washington, Martin

Luther King, and others are reviewed. But many of the alternative views insist that there is no obligation at all and that it is foolishness risking one's "sacred honor" if one's own skin would be threatened in the process.

Well, then, is the answer perfect freedom? But what is freedom? Is it a state of nature, and is that sustainable? What is the role of property and justice? Is it a laissez faire market? Or is the market "perfect competition" or "creative destruction"? Or is it rule of law? Or is it something else more personal? Whatever it is, extensive Freedom House and World Bank data show political liberty, economic freedom, markets, and rule of law go together—and all of these tend to concentrate in the West. But why, then, does every critic believe that America and the West are in crisis? Senator Daniel Patrick Moynihan and many others are mustered to reinforce the belief that there is decay even if there is little agreement on the cause or what to do about it.

The next three chapters consider the standard remedies proposed by critics and adopted by governments to solve the problems of decay. Equality is probably the hardiest of the three alternative ideals aimed against the more commonsensical values of the West. Many questions are raised about what is equality, how it might relate to freedom, and what the benefits and costs of different definitions might be? Or is justice the goal, as Plato argued? The friendlier challenge is the progressive one to aim simply for social justice, since pure equality and strict justice seem unattainable. Again, many issues are raised for the reader to consider regarding what justice might mean, what would be required to achieve it, and what the costs to American values might be, if any. Or is the response to decay simple hard work and conventional social conformity? Is Eric Hoffer correct that ordinary work and average people's daily life can substitute for a consideration of deeper values, especially for duty and responsibility? Or is work its own reward, perhaps the only reward? Or is duty necessary to justify work and even possibly intellectually defensible? The play *Other Peoples' Money* is used as the source for many related critical questions.

All is brought together in an investigation of Western values that has a traditionalist bent but still leaves the largest questions open for the reader to contemplate, including whether it will in fact survive. There is clearly room to conclude that it will not, unless its people choose that it will.

Citations are kept to a minimum. The inquisitive reader, however, will have sufficient guidance from those utilized to follow the themes further, especially if pursued through the additional footnotes in the author's own referenced works. All of the major selections from the classical works cited here can be found in a book of readings available through the Bellevue University Press titled, *Western Vision and American Values: The Kirkpatrick Signature Series Reader*. Bellevue University professors Tony Jasnowski, Clif Mason,

Del Stites, and Joseph Wydeven co-edited that work with the author, and their involvement obviously has influenced the composition of this work. I would also like to express my appreciation to Robert Moffit and professors Tom Myers, Judd Patton, Sung Pae, Ed Rauchut, and all of my students at Bellevue University during the three years consumed in this project for inspiring this book. Of course, none of them are responsible for its failings.

The goal of the book before you is to tell the story of the Western vision and its American values and institutions in a simple, easily communicable manner to a nation that is quickly losing an understanding of its roots. What has been unique about this quest for the author has been the commitment to it by a university that had earlier required a course based upon this general theme, but was very supportive of stretching its understanding and developing its view of citizenship even further. I wish particularly to thank John Muller, its president, and Berniece and William Grewcock for the time and opportunity they gave me to reflect upon the state of the West and to write my views about its condition and what would be necessary to sustain it.

Donald J. Devine, Bellevue University

Chapter One

Contesting World Traditions

WHY VALUES?

On September 11, 2001, when two airplanes destroyed the World Trade Center towers, another hit the Pentagon, and a fourth probably aimed at the Capitol crashed in Pennsylvania, no more terrible manifestation could be imagined of how holding different values can have momentous consequences. Muslim fundamentalists' beliefs led the terrorists to see the United States as their Satanic enemy and view its values as a threat to their values. The mechanisms used—the lives of 19 men and aircraft turned into makeshift missiles—were primitive, but this was enough to destroy sophisticated buildings and many innocent lives. In a real sense, *it was their values that were the critical weapon.* Consequently, no one can truly understand the world they live in unless they understand other peoples' traditions and values.

But these tragic events also revealed something about the values and traditions of the American people—expressed in the courage, compassion, patriotism, and generosity that were demonstrated during that crisis by those who charged the hijackers on the Pennsylvania flight, and the firemen, policemen, doctors, nurses, rescue workers, and ordinary citizens who pitched in for the rescue efforts. The immediately following threat of biological warfare from anthrax-filled letters in Washington, D.C., called for values like resourcefulness, technological expertise, energy, independence, and concern for neighbor. As it is important to understand others, it is just as or more important to understand American values, how they were developed, and the institutions that support them.

Yet, these are big issues and most of us live our personal lives in a narrower world of family, work, community, associations, and leisure. It is also critical

1

to understand everyday events and how values affect them—to reflect upon how and why we act or do not interact with the people we come into contact with each day, how one deals with family obligations, work responsibilities and civic life generally

How does one, how do you, decide questions about values?

—Is it possible to judge each occurrence on the facts or is some standard necessary?

—What standards or values can or should be used?

—Which standards, values, or tradition do you rely upon?

EVERYONE HAS A TRADITION

Consider. You, like everyone, have received values from some tradition, even if it has been rejected sometime thereafter. Tradition sets assumptions about things and gives meaning to individual and social life, more or less successfully, at least initially. Usually, it is learned from one's parents and family. Understanding, defending, or criticizing tradition does not require formal training. Its beliefs are transmitted as the common sense of the family and/or larger local grouping and is defended or criticized on common-sense grounds. All questions asked of traditionalists, therefore, are answered "naturally" as if the respondent had never been exposed to formal higher education or philosophy. Responses simply draw out what the traditionalist already thinks. If the tradition of one's birth is rejected, another must be substituted—even if that is neutrality between all things (if that is possible). Self-interest can be a standard or even self-generated values, in some logical or illogical form, can be utilized. All of these can be called traditions. Some set of beliefs is required to sort through a very busy reality, representing the billions of pieces of sense data surrounding us. Relying upon these roughly formed sets of values is what normal people do naturally, acting within their culture and/or civilization through institutions, groups, and themselves individually.[1]

As you have a tradition, so do others. To understand your planet, it is necessary to know how others see the world too. Let us investigate them and start with perhaps the earliest tradition, the one called The People, or as the Native American Eagle Man referred to it, *The People who "were always here"* tradition.[2] The tribe, the clan, the native people tend to lead an isolated way of life always in one general locale, basically unaware of other traditions—so, naturally, they consider and label themselves the only people of the world. They live all life "within the great, complete beauty" of the Mother Earth and the Great Spirit that exist immediately with and among them. Literally, as the American native peoples believed, "Mother Earth is our real mother, because every bit of us truly comes from her and daily she takes care of us," including at the end of life in a "much higher plane beyond" but without hell fire. Individuals are respected, but only "providing that individual freedom does not threaten the tribe or the people or Mother Earth." Nature is primary; she is benign; she does not end but is in an "eternal circle," where everything is "truly holy." In this nature around us, "we are all related" land, mountains, rivers, weather, animals, and plant-life. This entire "holy people" is to live in harmony with nature taking only what "you need to exist." This life is only threatened by exploitation and migration from the outside.

Aldo Leopold presents a modern version of this perspective, by demanding that "soils, waters, plants, animals" must stop being viewed as property, as in the West and be thought of as "fellow members" of the community, as was the case among the native Peoples. All people must act more simply in their lives, more "here" in the sacred environment of modern times, the same as in ancient days. Nature does include all humans, animals, and plant life, and it is the equal obligation of all to respect each other.[3] Sociologist David Maybury-Lewis, generally favorable to the tribal tradition, mentions some of the trade-offs demanded by this tradition, primarily initiation rights such as male and female sex mutilation, the learning value of the infliction of pain and anxiety by the tribe, and the necessity for conformity.[4] In the extreme case of conformity to a tradition, a community could so blindly follow its tradition that it could randomly kill fellow members of the people, as depicted in the popular short story *The Lottery*.[5] Although this is fiction, many traditional peoples did practice human sacrifice.

Hinduism is a Western name for innumerable sects in the Indus River Valley holding varying versions of a mixture of Aryan and native traditions. Originating about 1500 B.C, there is no fixed cannon for Hinduism but the Veda is very ancient and the Upanishads were a later central holy book added by the Brahmanists, whose formulation is the foundation of modern Hindu doctrine. It views nature as much more capricious than do the "always here" peoples. Rather than the acceptance of a benign nature, the goal is liberation from a relentless and perverse nature and the cycle of rebirth and suffering brought about by it and one's own actions. For an individual, through prayer (yoga) and moving up through a caste structure, it is possible to escape and find peace by re-unifying with nature's universal soul.[6] Failure to escape nature, however, often results in *fatalism* since it is very difficult to reject nature while living in it. One doctrine, suttee—the religious obligation for a widow to immolate herself at her husband's death—could not survive in India even after the British rule and law that eliminated it had ended. But the basic tradition, modified somewhat by Mongol and English law, still prospers so that, today, Hinduism is the third largest religious tradition, with 900 million adherents, still mostly in India.

Buddha was raised in the "always here" tradition about 500 B.C. and was additionally isolated from worldly difficulties by his wealth as a young prince, but when he encountered evil he was so shocked that he devoted his life to confronting it. After first following a severe Brahman-like lifestyle to overcome it, he adopted the *Middle Way* based both upon meditation (as with Hindu priests) but also with observing moral precepts in everyday life. The Way has four "noble truths"—existence is suffering in repeated cycles of birth and death, the cause of suffering is emotional attachment, suffering can end in a state called Nirvana, and Nirvana can be found by an individual following the "noble path" of right, moral views. The emphasis is upon being gentle, denying self, and compassion for others.[7] It spread from Nepal and India to China, Japan, Thailand, and Burma, among other Asian nations, where it had great impact. The Chinese and Japanese civilizations adopted major aspects of the Way, but this was also mixed with indigenous and competing local religions into these great civilizations of the East. China's tradition has been significantly modified by communism and Japan's by the Western occupation following World War II, but the Middle Way still influences how hundreds of millions of people in the region think and act today.

A fourth tradition, *Judaism*, uniquely saw life as an integrated story, with a beginning, middle, and potential end, the first to deny that nature was cyclical. Rather than the cycle of eternal return found in all of the other early major traditions (even by the philosopher Plato, in the *Meno*), the Jews saw *history in a linear manner*—stretching from the creation of the world by an eternal, personal, and just God, through Adam and the generations, to Abraham, Isaac, and Jacob and the Egyptian sojourn, to the liberation by God of his people, the occupation of Israel, the judges and then kings, the captivity, the re-occupation, the destruction of Jerusalem and the dispersion, down to today. In an important sense, history was invented by the Jews.[8] Creation is God's first act for human history. Indeed, the idea of the single Creator comes from Judaism. Man acts through history, either following God's law of justice or by following his own selfish interests to destruction. Historically, the Jews existed, not primarily as isolated individuals, but as the Chosen People. As such, they were to testify to the fact of a unitary God acting in history, one who demanded that His creatures act with His justice for the good of His community. His people fell many times as a result of not following His law, but each time have risen again as His witness to the world, which ultimately will be unified in peace under a Messiah or anointed leader. A great empire under David and Solomon, today it has a moderately sized but very influential "Diaspora" almost everywhere, but only one relatively small and often endangered state, Israel.

Christianity grew from Judaism and was the major means of transmitting its ideas into a widespread civilization. Christianity continues the importance of history by starting with the same Creator and making the whole Jewish tradition a means for the ultimate arrival of a Messiah, who is changed from a ruler to a suffering servant of God. A man called Jesus claimed to be this Messiah for whom the Jews were waiting for salvation—not to change its law but to fulfill it. As recorded by Matthew, however, He taught that the justice of the Old Testament is not sufficient, but that individuals must be more than just, to be merciful, even to be "perfect as your heavenly Father is perfect."[9] The goal of perfection makes individual holiness the supreme value even surpassing justice—to go even to the extreme length of throwing off body parts if they will lead to sin. These individuals have the obligation to the community, to neighbors, to love them as themselves. While its adherents may fall into sin, Jesus' grace is believed to be sufficient for forgiveness and future redemption in Heaven. In modern times, its best-selling author, C. S. Lewis, even makes history the judge of Christ's mission to the world. The world does not have the option to say Jesus was just a good teacher or moral thinker. Either this man was in fact God [technically a "person" of God, with the Father and Holy Spirit, in a Trinity] and rose from the dead or he was a "lunatic— on the level with the man who says he is a poached egg—or else he would be the Devil of Hell."[10] If He was God, all have the moral obligation to search for him and follow his teaching, no matter how difficult, although He also said He would make it easy for those who chose to follow Him to the Father.

Islam (submission or acceptance) finds Christianity wrong to place individual holiness above the social justice of God's community. Instead, both holiness and justice are one, as are all aspects of life under the one (not triune) Allah, the One (true) God. He spoke through the Jewish and Christian prophets (especially Abraham) but found His true prophet in Muhammad, who established the perfect law of Islam, beginning in Arabia in 622 A.D. As the later great collator of Islam's teachings, al-Shafi'i summarized its doctrine, "On all matters touching the Muslim, there is either a binding decision (based upon the Quran [holy book] or the tradition) or an indication to the right answer."[11] All knowledge and decisions, therefore, derive from Islamic law, or *Shari'a*. The goal of the Muslim is to praise Allah and submit to the law. Unlike Christianity and—to a lesser extent—Judaism, the holy state leader is to unify mosque and state, with the religious subject to the state, unless the state abandons Allah and the law. Indeed, in Islam, only the Muslim can be a true citizen. Although some early Islamic regimes practiced some toleration of the "people of the book" (primarily Jews and Christians), these could not fully participate in the state.

The reason outside participation is limited in Islam is that the state must be holy, so only believers can truly serve it. Thus, non-believers defile a holy state. Likewise, converting to other religions those who already believe is subverting the state. While Christianity has often been allied with the government and aimed to make it more holy, the state has always been viewed as a possible threat to the church and always profane. It was Jesus who divided what was due to Caesar from what was due to God. The Muslim unification of Allah and the state was so powerful and so inspired its adherents that it almost conquered the world, barely being stopped in Western Europe as late as the 17th century. As it was, it spread from the Arab world to Greece, the Balkans, the Middle East, and the Orient (Indonesia has the largest number, 170 million), including India (103 million, and whose minority rule of it was not changed until the British arrived in the 19th century). Indeed, most of Asia remains primarily Muslim, outside China and Japan. Islam remains very vital, with the world's largest population growth, and is very protective of its interests. There are about 1.3 billion Muslims (compared to 2 billion Christians), with two major branches, Sunni (83%) and Shi'ah (16%).

FOUR MORE MODERN WESTERN TRADITIONS

Not all traditions are purely spiritual or religious. Some people identify more with modern traditions that mix religious values with non-religious ones, adopting partially or wholly secular traditions. We will consider four here. *Conservative* traditions include religious and national elements, in the United States primarily Christianity mixed with American local customs and the founding principles of the Constitution. The modern conservative tradition can be identified with the scholar, Russell Kirk.[12] He believed that modern America was "using up the moral and intellectual capital which had been accumulated" over the ages from the Judeo-Christian tradition and that the job of the modern conservative was to "restore consciousness among men to the worth of tradition." For only tradition can raise men and women "above the brutes." He found America's tradition, its spiritual heritage and local ways of life, under attack and was concerned whether it "will be drained dry within a very few decades" unless some leaders arise to make it alive for the next generations. To him, this revival must be accomplished primarily by acting through the community, the family, and the church rather than through government. Government is bureaucratic rather than creative and, in any event, Constitutional government itself cannot persist without the moral support of these institutions and the values upon which they are based. Indeed, in recent years, as government has expanded beyond the limited role set by America's Founders, it has become part of the problem. Without the revival of the traditional values, a humane limited government and a moral society will become impossible for the United States.

To a great extent, American conservatism was a reaction to the great success of modern *progressivism*. Late 19th century English liberal thinkers T. H. Green and Leonard Hobhouse rejected the traditional conservative fear of government power, denying that government should have only the limited power of preventing internal and foreign coercion, what they considered a narrow "negative" view of liberty. Rather, they argued, government power could also be harnessed to positively promote freedom and social welfare. "Positive" freedom would allow government to use its power for good ends, although for secular purposes, not for religious ones. The idea of expanded national government power harnessed to perform good works greatly influenced Woodrow Wilson and Franklin Roosevelt in the U.S., which led to many new national government programs during their and following administrations. To confront the recent popular reaction against this more active government, there has been a progressive reappraisal. Noted journalist and inspiration for the New Democrat, E. J. Dionne, Jr., concedes that progressives have "foolishly" often cast themselves in favor of "coercion and bureaucracy" rather than for freedom. The modern formulation for the "liberal" or, as he prefers, true progressive tradition in America is to resurrect the original idea of positive freedom to define its doctrine. Progressives, today, must respect the tradition that government must have some limits or government can become invasive of individual liberty. But positive government action is often required that goes well beyond the traditional governmental functions, and most Americans now accept that reality. But for success in 21st century America, progressives must be able to explain why new governmental action beyond the traditional scope will promote a greater positive liberty for the people.[13]

Many modern intellectuals go much further and reject the very idea of tradition itself. Noted 19th century thinker Ralph Waldo Emerson rejected tradition absolutely. All individual decisions should be based upon *one's own values*. The community must not be the source of values—indeed, it suppresses the true values of individuals through the heavy hand of enforced conformity and communal sympathy. Rather, convention and empathy should be replaced by "truth and health in rough electric shocks." Only the individual on his own, in his own mind, can be a moral source. His single moral injunction is simply "obey your heart." To him, "nothing is at last sacred but the integrity of your own mind."[14] Twentieth century writer, Albert Camus, likewise rejected tradition and any idea of sacredness of the individual. He believed that the individual was totally alone and so the only possible moral source. He was more fatalistic than Emerson about life and nature, which he saw merely as unceasing labor, mitigated only by "the *higher fidelity that negates the gods and raises rocks.*"[15] One can be heroic in the face of this difficult truth—the only truth—by simply forging ahead, realizing everything else is illusion. To the extent that either self-reliance or heroic fatalism are not philosophically derived but are learned, they too may be considered traditions.

These ten traditions cover most of the peoples of the world—East, West, and in between. There are, of course, variations upon them—for example, Protestants and Catholics under the general category of Christianity or Sunni and Shi'ah under Islam—but these basic value systems set the general framework within which most individuals perceive the world around them. Which one formed your early consciousness? Which one do you identify with today? Does that tradition provide a satisfying view of the world to you? Would you consider another alternative?

What difference do these world traditions make? Most people do rely upon one of these traditions and are reasonably satisfied with them. They affect how we live our daily lives within our nations. Should women cover their whole body from head to toe, only their heads, just their private parts, or nothing at all? To a great degree, tradition sets the standard. Must men let their beards grow, or are they considered barbarian if they do not shave, or do they shave their heads as well? Do people follow customs or the law or their own whims? Do they follow a religion associated with the state or one separate from it or none?

In the United States, the dominant tradition is Christianity, but there are secular influences as well. Judaism, too, has thrived in America from its earliest days and has had an influential voice in its affairs almost as long. More precisely, according to an April 2001 survey by The Pew Research Center, 82 percent of Americans considered themselves Christian (53% Protestant—29% evangelical and 22% mainline—23% Roman Catholic and 6% other Christians), 4 percent were of non-Christian religions, 3 percent called themselves atheist or agnostic, and 11 percent refused to choose among the categories. Nearly two-thirds said their religion was "very" important in their own lives, belief in God was near unanimous, and nine in ten said they pray at least once a week, but most also believe that the church should be separate from the state and that all believers must respect the secular law.[16] Only a few nations worldwide even broadly share this mix of beliefs, predominately limited to Europe—from which the American tradition was developed—and South America and a few other outposts, which also received many of these same influences from the same source. It is this set of nations that is usually referred to as the West.

TRADITIONS IN CONFLICT

Tradition likewise affects how we relate to other nations. Because nations see the world through their own different traditional beliefs, they often come in conflict with each other: The People resisting outsiders, Hindu against Buddhist, Muslim in opposition to Jew, secular verses Christian, and so forth. To see how the values of the different traditions can influence each other over long periods of time, there is no better example than the conflict between Islam and Christianity. It began centuries before anyone ever heard of Osama bin Laden, precisely way back in the year 637.[17] At the time, Jerusalem had been under Christian rule and in intermittent peace (most recently interrupted by the Persians) for 300 years. But in that year, Jerusalem was assaulted and captured under the second caliph Omar. Few inhabitants there knew Islam, for this was only five years after Muhammad's death, and the Romans and Byzantines did not allow Jews to settle there for generations; so the assault was hardly reprisal but was an expression of the dynamism and zeal of the new faith for more adherents. For a while, the Muslims tolerated the majority Christians, but "toleration" did not include citizenship, which was forbidden to infidels. After the Fatimite (Arab) caliph Harkim took power, however, he ended the Christian pilgrimages and, in the year 1010, began violently persecuting Christians, including profaning and destroying their number one religious site, the Holy Sepulcher, Jesus' (temporary) tomb.

But the West ignored it. After the Seljuks overthrew the Fatimites, these Turkish Muslims decisively defeated the Christian Byzantine emperor Romanus IV at Manzikert in 1071, threatening the entire Eastern Empire. Emperor Alexius I appealed for help. This provocation finally convinced Pope Urban II and the Council of Clermont in 1095 to launch a crusade from the West to rescue the beleaguered Christians of Jerusalem and the Byzantine East generally, and to restore the Sepulcher. The first crusade won Jerusalem in 1099—which became the capital of the Latin Kingdom of Jerusalem, which lasted almost 200 years. In a series of eight more crusades—some provoked, some not—the Christians established multiple fiefs in the Middle East, collectively called the Outremer—the West beyond the seas—states. The Muslims of Damascus, Cairo, and Baghdad initially were more interested in fighting each other, but finally, Saladin united them and reclaimed Jerusalem in 1187. But the last Christian stronghold, Acre, did not fall until 1291. It was a long fight but Islam finally expelled the Christians from the Outremer.

The assault upon Jerusalem and Byzantium was by no means the most important to the West. In the year 711, long before the crusades, a Muslim army under Tarik had attacked Spain and ultimately expelled the armed Christian survivors into the remote northwestern corner of the peninsula. The Moor army then crossed the Pyrenees and was not stopped in Western Europe until Tours in Southern France, in 732—fighting an Arab-based civilization in the middle of Christendom. It was a close call, with Europe barely surviving with all of the advantages of terrain and supply under a motley force organized by king Charles Martel. Spain did not begin its Christian reconquest until 1061 and was not generally successful in dislodging the Muslims from Western Europe until 1492, nor was fully successful until 1609.

But the greatest threat was in Southeastern Europe.[18] After constant battle, Ottoman Turks finally conquered the Eastern Christian capital, Constantinople, in 1453 and completely destroyed Western influence in the Mideast. Almost all of the early Christian areas of the Levant were converted through force and preference, with few traces even remaining today. These Muslims were not stopped from controlling all of Central Europe until 1571 at the sea battle of Lepanto and—decisively—in 1683 at Vienna, by the last-minute arrival of John Sobieski to reverse a looming defeat. In other words, Islam was not finally stopped in Europe until America was settled. Slowly, the tide turned as the West grew stronger and Islam more rigid. By the 18th century, Europe (but not the U.S.) was now occupying Muslim states and re-creating Outremer. The Ottoman Empire fell after World War I, leaving no Muslim world power. While colonialism ended after World War II, the last Outremer state, Israel, remained as an irritant, while the West strongly outdistanced Islam economically and militarily. By the 21st century, in Sudan, Nigeria, Egypt, Indonesia, and other Muslin states, events turned again—now with local Christian populations previously protected under colonialism being persecuted in large numbers by Islamic states with little Western notice or reaction.

CONFLICT IN MODERN TIMES

For 1,000 years in three massive waves that almost broke Christendom entirely, Islam was the epitome of dynamism. During this time, the West simply held on or supported outposts. Over the next 300 years, the West was the more aggressive. The slow rise of Christianity and the rapid rise of Islam is one of history's dramatic divergences, with the former starting a half millennium earlier than Islam but not reaching maturity until a full millennium after. Once on the offense, Christian forces sacked Jerusalem and killed all of the Muslims and the Jews supporting them in the first crusade. There were even incidents against Jews in Europe. By far the worst was during the first crusade when Count Emich of Leniningen massacred hundreds of Jews in Worms and Speyer—although in both cases the local bishops sheltered area Jews in their castles, preventing worse abuse. The Crusaders were equal opportunity despoilers, seizing Tanis in the second crusade, killing Coptic Christians. During the fourth crusade, the Franks and Venetians actually sacked the seat of the Eastern Christian Empire, Constantinople—wantonly killing Christians—weakening it for the Turks. Sadly, pretty much everyone did the same to non-combatants in those tough times including the Saracens at Acre and Antioch and the Fatamids and Seljuks often, mostly against each other. Saladin and St. Louis were rare exceptions. Whatever the excesses, by the late 17th century, Western arms became dominant, with none of its homeland territory being occupied except temporarily by a non-Western power down to this very day.

But Western freedom from assault from outside traditions did not mean security or peace. Religious wars between Catholics and Protestants beginning in the 16th century, the French Revolution-inspired secular Napoleonic wars against monarchical authority in the 18th century, the American Civil War between regional democratic states, and the modern government World Wars I and II, although mostly interrupted by long intervals of peace, all resulted in mass destruction and many Western deaths. A new phenomenon of state mass-killing of their own populations by new secular traditions resulted in the Nazis holocaust slaughtering millions of Jews and the Soviet Union and the Peoples' Republic of China murdering tens of millions more of their own citizens.[19] While these ideologies weakened or disappeared by the end of the 20th century, Islam was stirring again. Islamic values were in active conflict with Jewish ones in the Middle East, Hindu ones on the Indian subcontinent, and Han ones in Indonesia and Western China. In the past decade, there have been a dozen—not including Osama bin Laden's 9/11 carnage—confirmed terrorist attacks by fundamentalist Muslims against American targets alone. While these have been acts of terrorism, the weapon of the weak, not full-scale war, one suspects the 1,300 year conflict between the two largest world religious traditions will not end with bin Laden.

Most Muslims are non-violent. Because the Quran makes the state holy, however, Islam cannot easily allow non-Muslims to become citizens even under more tolerant regimes and remain true to its doctrine. Without full participation in the state, non-citizens are under pressure to convert or be passive. As a result, the earliest centers of Christianity in Anatolia today have almost no remaining Christians. Where significant Christian communities persisted (and, therefore, were considered as a threat), they were always tolerated only as simple peasants or worse (as in Spain and the Balkans) unless they converted. Jews, being much less numerous and more educated, generally were treated more tolerantly. Conversions from Islam, since subversive, could not be tolerated even from the people of the book and attempts to do so could be punished by death. Yet, Jesus' final demand to his followers required Christians to make attempts to convert, even if gently. Just before the 9/11 tragedy, two Americans (and others) were arrested in Afghanistan for trying to teach Christianity. The Afghans were threatened with death and the Americans with

imprisonment until they were rescued by U.S. and alliance forces, which had
to overthrow the fundamentalist regime to do so. Christian missionaries have
been assassinated in many Islamic nations in recent times and even Western
allies like Saudi Arabia impose death for conversions. Consequently, refusing
to accept non-Muslims as citizens within Islamic states remains an enduring
source of tension between it and the West.

The American political scientist, Samuel P. Huntington, in his book, *The
Clash of Civilizations and the Remaking of the World Order*, published in
1996, found by actual count of world conflicts that Islam had the most difficulty living in peace with its neighbors. He predicted that the conflict between
Islam and the West would be the predominant world rivalry in the 21st century, years before the 9/11 attack.[20] The case of Turkey demonstrates that the
relationship need not be antagonistic, since that Muslim nation is a major U.S.
ally in the North Atlantic Treaty Organization. Yet, many Muslim institutions
had to be moderated by an aggressive Westernizing, secular military in order
to integrate believers into the secular state and many Muslims in Turkey resent that weakening.[21] In the most recent elections, the secular political parties were overwhelmingly defeated by a party more sympathetic to Islamic
ideals. While the new party professes to be committed to secular government,
it is clear that a religious revival has taken place across the Islamic world, and
it is not clear what will be the consequences.

THE CHALLENGE

As the West faces a reinvigorated Islamic challenge from abroad, its religious
and traditional values seem questioned ever more widely within its own civilization. Its birthplace, Europe, especially, has seen momentous declines in
Christian church attendance and religious observance.[22] Indeed, many see a
"death of God" there, reflected in the loss of commitment to its once unques-
tioned Christian tradition, and the rise of secularism. Many moderns simply
cannot accept a tradition just because their ancestors did so in the past. Intellectuals, especially, scorn tradition and find its decline a positive social development assisting secular values like multiculturalism and societal diversity. With Emerson and Camus, it is clear that to them tradition is simply myth
and falsehood. It is a lie and does not deserve support.

Even modern American liberals and conservatives have reservations about
tradition. Dionne relies upon the legitimacy of tradition primarily only back
into the late 19th century. Even Kirk, the conservative, specifically rejects tradition as the only guide, supports dissent, and finds that there are bad traditions. This may be a more rational conservatism but it is no longer purely tra-

ditional. More problematically, while Kirk finds the Western tradition still valid, most of his fellow scholars question it. Indeed, by the 21st century, it is questionable whether true, unquestioning tradition exists at all to any significant degree in the West.

While many worldwide, and even in the United States, still simply accept some tradition as a given, modern life and communication clearly work against accepting beliefs just because one's family does. Modern people demand reasons. Don't you? If one is to truly understand one's world, it is necessary to take a closer look at tradition—as we will do in the following section—using reason and scientific analysis to explore it further.

NOTES

1. Alfred Krober and Clyde Kluckhohm, *Culture* (New York: Random House, 1952). Also see Donald J. Devine, *The Political Culture of the United States* (Boston: Little Brown, 1972), chap. 1.

2. Eagle Man, "We Are All Related," in Ed McGaa, ed., *Mother Earth Spirituality*, (New York: Harper-Collins, 1990).

3. Aldo Leopold, *A Sand Country Almanac* (New York: Oxford University Press, 1949).

4. David Maybury-Lewis, "Tribal Wisdom," in *Millennium* (London: Biniman, 1992).

5. Shirley Jackson, *The Lottery* (New York: Farrar, Strauss & Giroux, 1976).

6. E. Hume, trans. "Katha Upanishad," in *The Thirteen Upanishads* (London: Oxford University Press, 1931).

7. Buddha, "The First Sermon," in Edward J. Thomas, ed., *The Life of Buddha* (London: Routledge, 1927).

8. Herbert Butterfield, "Originality of the Old Testament," in C. Thomas McIntire, ed., *Writings on Christianity and History* (New York: Oxford University Press, 1979) and Paul Johnson, *A History of the Jews* (New York: Harper & Row, 1987).

9. The Gospel of St. Matthew; Rodney Stark, *The Rise of Christianity* (San Francisco: Harper-Collins, 1996); Judith Herrin, *The Formation of Christendom* (Princeton: Princeton University Press, 1987); Richard Fletcher, *The Barbarian Conversion* (New York: Henry Holt, 1997); Robin Lane Fox, *Pagans and Christians* (New York: Knopf, 1986).

10. C. S. Lewis, *Mere Christianity* (New York: Macmillan, 1943), II: 3.

11. Shafi'i "Treatise on the Roots of Jurisprudence," in F. E. Peters, ed., *Judaism, Christianity and Islam* (Princeton: Princeton University Press, 1990), 306–7; V. S. Naipaul, *Among the Believers* (New York: Random House, 1981).

12. Russell Kirk, *A Program for Conservatives* (Washington, D.C.: Regnery, 1954).

13. E. J. Dionne, "Progressive Promise," in *They Only Look Dead* (New York: Simon and Schuster, 1997), iv and 9.

14. Ralph Waldo Emerson, "Self-Reliance," in *Essays* (Boston: Munne, 1841).

15. Albert Camus, "The Myth of Sisyphus," in *The Myth of Sisyphus and Other Essays* (New York: Knopf, 1955).

16. The Pew Research Center, *American Views on Religion, Politics and Public Policy*, (Washington, D.C.: 2001), 38. These religious views have not changed much over time; compare Devine, *The Political Culture of the United States*, 222–28.

17. Malcolm Billings, *The Crusades* (New York: Sterling, 1996); Amin Maalouf, *The Crusades Through Arab Eyes* (New York: Shoeken Books, 1984); Andrew Sinclair, *Jerusalem: The Endless Crusade* (New York: Crown, 1995); and John Julius Norwich, *Byzantium: The Early Years* (New York: Knopf, 1996) and *Decline and Fall* (New York: Knopf, 1996).

18. Lord Kinross, *The Ottoman Centuries* (New York: Harper-Collins, 2000).

19. R. J. Rummel, *Death by Government* (New Brunswick, N.J.: Transaction, 1996), 121.

20. Samuel P. Huntington, *The Clash of Civilizations and the Remaking of the World Order*, (New York: Simon & Schuster, 1996). See also Fareed Zakaria, *The Future of Freedom* (New York: Norton, 2003), 126–32. Zakaria claims the roots go only 40 years, not 400 and that the issue is the Arab world and history, not Islam generally. Yet, even he admits the problem has "infected not just other Arab societies but countries outside the Arab world," and all of the other nations that he mentions are Islamic, with very few Muslim nations listed as exceptions, (145–46).

21. Andrew Mango, *Ataturk* (New York: Overlook, 2002).

22. The Pew Research Center, Pew Global Attitudes Project, December 2002, <http://*www.people-press.org*> (December 2002).

Chapter Two

Making Tradition
Rational and Scientific

IS YOUR TRADITION TRUE?

In the beginning, it is clear that we see the world the way our tradition tells us how to see it. A child is too young to question except in a superficial manner. So for the early years, tradition shapes reality for us. But as we gradually come into contact with the outside world, our traditions can be questioned. Outsiders doubt our previously unchallenged ways of living—our family relationships, how we dress, our sexual customs, the nutritional values of our traditional foods, how we pray and work, and even the accuracy of our holy books and our founding documents.

As long as people were protected from the outside world, tradition determined everything. Each local People held their own set of values that constituted their understanding of their world, learned within the family and the group. With some geographical isolation and limited external influences— little migration, commerce, and communication—alternate views hardly existed. So most of the early major world traditions developed almost complete unanimity of support for their values within their cultures. Commerce changed this, with traders coming from foreign regions to sell seemingly value-neutral and non-threatening material goods. But the camels, horses, ships, and armies brought new ideas with them, including the values of work, property, and culture that made the production and marketing of the new goods possible in the trading nation. That is why the story of tradition starts with the people who "were always here." They were always there so no one knew any alternative. But once trade or migration or both arrive, there are alternatives and questions.

The problem with new points of view is that each tradition has different inherent problems and they are sure to be raised to the light of day by outsiders. Each tradition has a major value but that value can be questioned in some manner that the tradition finds challenging to resolve. Each has a response, but the riposte is commonsensical, resting only upon the assumptions and mores of its own tradition.

The People Always Here confront new ideas by expecting that everyone simply must accept its values—as all have done within the tribe since time immemorial. All simply must see that reality is sacred and must be respected. In the extreme, tradition simply tries to keep all outside forces outside. Hinduism seeks to elude difficulties and answers the problem that only the best can escape from this world through meditation with the response that all should persevere to escape sooner or later. Buddhism, Judaism and Christianity are similar in that they respond that people need to pray and/or work and/or sacrifice more to resolve the difficulties created by new ideas and problems. Islam responds that making the state holy to solve new problems might be difficult, but the good community will repair to the law and overcome any threat. Conservatism likewise says to strive harder to preserve tradition, while progressivism insists leaders can positively adjust to new forces and still stay true to its values. When faced with the problem that there are evil selves, like Adolph Hitler, the self-reliant say it is not their fault that there are some bad hearts; the self-reliant are only responsible for their own. Lifting rocks may be a drag to many but that is all one can do anyway, responds the heroic fatalist. But common-sense answers like hope, persistence, prayer, work, adjustment, self-reliance, and perseverance do not satisfy many inquiring minds, as new questions are raised constantly.

PHILOSOPHY QUESTIONS HOW WE SEE—HOW DO WE SEE?

It is no coincidence that Socrates, considered the first philosopher, lived in Athens, the center of the Greek commercial world. From ancient Athens to today's World Trade Organization, new ideas arrive with trade, and tradition feels threatened. The first broad threat—when commercial Athens confronted new worlds and traditions—evoked the first systematic response, namely, philosophy. Philosophy, at bottom, is simply asking questions in a systematic form aimed at discovering what, in fact, is true. But merely asking questions in a dialogue can have a revolutionary effect on how we see the world. Philosophical questioning, however, must proceed in a rational manner, which Socrates explained by using the key examples of the cave and the slave.

Socrates' allegory of the cave pictures humanity—all of us—bound in the darkness so that we can only see a reflection of reality, as shadows projected from a fire to the wall of the cave.[1] The real things are hidden so that we only see the shadows that we think are real. Only through systematic questioning by a wise teacher dedicated to finding the truth can one reach the truth behind the reflections. Otherwise we think that what we see is reality, even though it is merely shadow. The slave is led out of the shadows by Socrates' careful questioning so well that he can even recall the complexities of geometry from his earlier existence in the cave.[2] Both the cave and the slave illustrate Socrates' major themes: Reality is hidden and can only be recalled by questioning from a dedicated teacher who can systematically lead people to the truth. What is apparent to people is what is taught to them through tradition in various communities. But they see only the shadows not the reality; the "ideal forms," the spiritual *essences*, are hidden behind them in the cave. Tradition may provide a satisfactory explanation to people, in one sense, but it is false. It does not reach reality but only the conventions of a people, which are distorted reflections from fundamental truth and underlying reality.

Socrates used the example of the ideal of the real rose, its essence, verses the corruptible reality that we see. This comparison shows no existing rose is rose, all the ones we see show some signs of underdevelopment or corruption; only the idea of it is rose, perfect, true, essential. Socrates discovered the Ideal, the concept, the real spiritual essence of the thing hidden behind the apparent reality of the tradition. Modern perception theory tends to confirm that we do not see directly but need mental processes to order perceptions.[3] Infants do constant testing of object separation from its background to distinguish size from movement. Some such mental decision is necessary or the child cannot even distinguish objects and so cannot succeed in using them in later life. Sailors, using reflexive sighting rules, perceive sails long before civilians can. Galileo's claim that the earth revolved around the sun was so difficult to prove because observation through telescopes demands certain mental protocols—you do not see planets move but infer motion. Ptolemaic navigation assumed the earth was the center and it was "proven" by its usefulness in successfully guiding sailors for centuries. Yet, its very success and reliability were what misled. Mental images certainly clarify sense data, why not precede them in being and importance, as Socrates and his student, disciple, and chronicler Plato argued?

If we could see through to the truth, we would understand that justice is the ideal that makes human life perfect. The spirit of justice requires that all be treated fairly while tradition's justice is what is good for the state, community, or people. Whether traditional values have been defined from time immemorial or interpreted by the people yesterday, they do not treat all people fairly or justly. The just society requires a just ruler—a philosopher king—who knows what is fair for all, just officials or guardians who will carry out just policy, and a just people who will follow them—rather than follow the myths taught to them by society's existing rulers and guardians, elected or not. Socrates taught his young students to rationally question tradition and authority and to reach for a society based on truth and justice; but Athens' governing democratic officials reacted by sentencing him to death for undermining the traditions of their people.[4]

THE IDEAL REPUBLIC?

How could anyone object to a society that was dedicated to treating all justly? What would the ideal rational republic look like without the distortions of tradition? Plato outlined the steps that would be necessary to transform a world of "real" (i.e., tradition-dominated) human beings into a world of true (ideal) human justice in his book *The Republic.*[5] Although undoubtedly based upon Socrates' thought, *The Republic* is probably more Plato than Socrates. It used the concept of the ideal to expound upon the qualities of the ideal state or republic and subtly upon the qualities of the perfect soul. He used rational questioning guided by "right reason" as a means to get through the distortions of self-interest, community myth, state power, and intellectual sophism. Deriving conclusions from reality rather than shadows, especially the ideal of good and justice for all, he described the perfectly just state that should be the model for all. As one conclusion, he rejected tradition by being the first to declare the justice of perfect equality between the sexes—now generally accepted by modern people centuries later as obviously true.

But right thinking follows through to the truth no matter how disturbing this is to one's traditional (or modern) beliefs. So *The Republic* also planned state arrangement of marriages, communal sharing of spouses, state rearing of children without parents even knowing their offspring, communal sharing of property under control of the state, rearing all children for war and sacrifice for the state, exposing deformed or sickly children to their deaths so they are not a burden on the state nor on creative individuals, allowing slavery (except not of fellow Greeks), and rule by a philosopher king rather than by the people. These may sound radical but does not the modern state set the rules for marriage such as no fault divorce, restrictions that "arrange" the results to some degree? Do not moderns share spouses somewhat in serial divorces? Do not state-sponsored day care and schooling constitute the rearing and training of children for state purposes? How different is abortion just before birth from exposing infants immediately after birth? Did not the U.S. once have slavery?

How does welfare from birth to grave and progressive taxation differ from communal sharing of resources? How is a strong president so different from a wise king? There are differences between all of these, of course, but each does suggest that Plato's reforms may not be so radical, at least not when some future generation perhaps looks back at us as we do on those who rejected sexual equality.

Plato did propose strong remedies because without this type of fundamental reform, perfect justice is impossible. For example, unless the state arranges and controls marriages and separates children from parents, certain families can accumulate power, money, brains, strength, beauty, or other qualities of birth and can pass them down to their children and future generations. This leads to inequality and unjust rewards for some over others. It leads to rule by the wealthy and powerful and handsome. If the republic is not given control over families, private power will create birth or merit aristocracies and sustain injustice and financial inequality. Justice requires that all power be given to the good republic so that it can do what is just for all. Naturally, the best people should lead this republic—those who know the ideal of the universal good and are willing to work to achieve it—and that is what the philosopher king is, the best one to rule. Why settle for less than the best? And he or she should have the best people for assistants (the guardians), obviously. The reason the world is such a sad place is that the worst rule, and even in democracies the demagogues fool and mislead the people. Put the right people with the right values in charge and give them the power, and one can achieve the just republic that all desire in their hearts. All that is necessary is the courage to act upon these convictions and adopt these essential reforms.

REAL HISTORY: FROM ARISTOTELIAN BALANCE TO MEDIEVAL SYNTHESIS

Plato did act, attempting to overthrow the decaying Athenian democratic state to create his just republic. He was one of the leaders of a cabal that tried, and he was forced to escape when it failed. Failure ultimately led to control by an unsophisticated Macedonian king who destroyed Athenian democracy anyway. Plato's student, Aristotle, was not surprised that what he considered extreme idealism resulted in unintended consequences. He found his teacher too abstract, too radical, too impractical. It probably is no coincidence that Aristotle worked for King Philip of Macedon and trained Alexander the Great—the practical representatives of the tradition. Aristotle combined philosophy and empirical science to balance both the abstract and the real in a more practical way, a mean or conjunction or dualism between the ideal and the material. He started with reality as it appeared, what is known best is closer to direct sense experience, he claimed, not to immaterial forms or ideals. "Objects nearer to sense are prior and better known," the opposite of Plato. Rather than questioning everything ruthlessly, Aristotle claimed it was impossible not to start somewhere—with some "pre-existent knowledge."[6] That is, philosophy must start with tradition. For many activities in life, that is enough.

For serious analysis, however, questioning of the type Socrates proposed is required. But Aristotle "invents" a systemic logic to do it even more formally. Yet, even logic is based upon assumptions (axioms or theses) derived from experience or tradition. Starting with axioms, he questions further with mathematics or deductive (syllogistic) or inductive (generals implicit in particulars) reasoning and empirical research. Both abstract and empirical duality must be investigated to fully perceive and understand the world we live in. Both spirit and matter constitute the whole. After careful examination, we really know something scientifically when we know its cause or deduce something from axioms using the rules of logic. Still, all reasoning must start somewhere or there is an "infinite regress," reasoning back forever to new first principles. To Aristotle, we know the axiom "beforehand but better than the conclusion." Questioning is necessary so we may learn, but it rests upon the sense data evident in the tradition. Therefore, what we see, although it can be misleading, is real not shadows and the slave is not recalling a mythical cave but is learning from his teacher.

Aristotle's more practical philosophy had consequences for the types of society and government he proposed. He believed that logic could be mastered by the normally intelligent and did not require the super intelligence of the philosopher king. So, government could be rule by the one (monarchy), by the few (oligarchy), or even by the many (democracy), although a king is usually more practical. All that is necessary is that the type of government match the traditions of the society, not that some flawless society be created to do everything perfectly. No radical transformations like those suggested by Plato are normally needed or desirable for the good society. All that is necessary is to properly train people in virtue, and the proper government can produce reasonable human happiness.

In fact, no ideal Republic was created. Real kings manipulating both material and spiritual forces ruled by power rather than right, as did Alexander the Great, who was followed for 700 years by a better-organized and even more pragmatic—but also more brutal—Roman state. Aristotle's pragmatism but not his virtue—especially in the later years of Rome—became the norm for the world rather than Plato's ideals. Power, not virtue, continued to rule the world. After a millennium, the Roman Empire fell also. Before it did, a new religion—Christianity—first was tolerated and then became its official religion. So, when Rome fell, it brought both state and church down into what have been called the "dark ages." Roman architectural achievements were destroyed or atrophied, agriculture and art declined, and social life disbursed from cities into small areas that could be defended to some degree or other from pillage by outside warlords. Slowly, the fiefs rising from the collapsed empire created internal order and new local institutions that joined the surviving church in creating a mixed Medieval social form based upon lord, church, and commoner.[7]

As these religious, local, and private property institutions slowly created a feudal order, stability promoted increased commerce, which began to produce better economic conditions. Even Aristotle was recovered from the more advanced Arab world and his thought basically dominated philosophic and political thought in Europe for the next 1,000 years—especially through Thomas Aquinas' synthesis of his philosophy with Christian theology, making it more "dualistic" even than the original. After a very long period of slowly increasing prosperity, learning was revived and colleges flourished, which led to new questioning in a period called the Renaissance. Reacting against the large gain of church property resulting from this relative prosperity and the laxity and abuse it promoted, a searching Protestantism rose and challenged the existing Roman church authorities, leading to the questioning of the whole medieval social order that had dominated Europe for so long.

A NEW WORLD ORDER OF REASON AND SCIENCE

Into this new, more questioning world strode a philosopher commanding enough to successfully challenge the great Aristotle. Rene Descartes objected to Aristotle as too accepting of first premises and the proof of it was the muddle of Thomistic reasoning by then. There were dual or different Scholastic interpretations of so many subjects that everything was in doubt—religion, learning, government, and social life generally. For certainty (and stability), a ruthless questioning of everything to determine the one certain truth must be substituted. Plato was correct that questioning must be radical, but it must be pursued more systematically. For Descartes, the method was analytic geometry—which he invented for the task—much more systematic than simple, probing Platonic dialogue.[8] While Descartes, aware of Socrates' fate, did not directly threaten the existing powers, his method probed everything and would finally disturb all tradition and authority. His approach found greatest support among his native country's intellectuals who, in the following century, provided the moral support for the French Revolution and the whole following European radical search for a single rational explanation of human social life.

At about the same time, Aristotle's scientific work was being questioned as not significantly experimental in form. Isaac Newton's work had demonstrated that too much of Aristotle's physics was accepted without close enough examination and sufficient testing. This challenge was promoted by the philosopher, Francis Bacon—who claimed to follow Aristotle—including a modified title for his major work *The New Organon*—but called for a more rigorous empirical science in the modern era. Following Aristotle rather than Descartes—whose physics he found inferior to Newton's—Bacon agreed that the sense data we see are the primary elements to be analyzed. One must start with "simple sensuous perception" as pure fact, for no one can see what is "behind" but only what was there. Bacon differed with Aristotle (who made them more-or-less equal) by claiming that sense data were superior to analytics, that the conclusions being discovered by science were better known than the axioms. One starts, then, with the data and proceeds inductively, "as if by machinery," every step of the investigation up through "progressive stages of certainty" to finding the truth.[9]

Bacon did not directly question the old philosophy for "cultivation" of nonphysical knowledge but he considered abstract philosophy, and by implication values, only "ornaments," secondary to material facts. Like Descartes, Bacon's potentially radical view was confined to the scientific world and did not directly threaten tradition or its representatives in the political realm. But the idea that material things were superior to values, truth, and ideals was to change things radically over the next two centuries. In the meantime, a Protestant Reformation, followed by a Catholic one and a peace that stabilized relations between the two, led to an explosion of artistic and commercial activity that resulted in an even more substantial prosperity for a new, more widespread middle class, which also promoted political reforms and more popular participation.[10]

THE SCIENTIFIC REPUBLIC?

But the middle classes were not the only ones stirring. After 200 years of scientific success in explaining the physical world, the dominant intellectual of modern times, Karl Marx, demanded that Newtonian science and Cartesian analysis be applied to understand and reform the social life of all human beings, of all classes equally. Science had decoded the material world and promoted progress but it ignored the social component of it, the more important part. It was time to throw aside Bacon's and Descartes' caution. Their questioning was not radical enough. For example, Descartes' geometry did not question all of social life but started with the apparent world as it was. Scientists more often than not even supported the "opiate" of the people, religion, including Newton himself, when science confirmed nothing of the sort. Even Plato's republic had spiritual and idealistic aspects.

Now that the scientific method had proven its superiority in rejecting spirits, ghosts, and myths and focusing upon real, material things, the scientific study of humanity must do the same. Rejecting the spiritual and ideal as unscientific, Marx substituted a strictly materialist explanation of social life. With no prior or metaphysical assumptions he could probe scientifically to the core reality underlying social life—both to understand the present and predict the future. He and his financial supporter and colleague Frederick Engels presented their findings in their scientific masterpiece "The Communist Manifesto."[11]

Its division of world history into Ancient, Feudal, Capitalist, and Modern won almost universal acceptance as the most parsimonious description of history possible. At each stage, one class dominated the other because it controlled the strategic productive property. This oppression would be repeated until the classes and the private property from which they derive their power are eliminated and all people are left equal. Capitalism is the final stage of this oppression. Contrary to popular prejudice and academic ignorance, however, Marx's scientific analysis even gave capitalism great credit for moving society ahead. "The bourgeoisie, during its rule of scarce one hundred years, has created more massive and more colossal productive forces than have all preceding generations together." Capitalism also deserved the credit for eliminating the earlier oppressive order. "It has pitilessly torn asunder the motley feudal ties that bound man to his 'natural superiors' and has left remaining no other nexus between man and man than naked self-interest, than callus 'cash payment.'"

Indeed, capitalism stripped "the halo from every occupation hitherto honored," priest, warrior, physician, lawyer, and poet. It has "torn away from the family its sentimental veil and has reduced the family relation to a mere money relation." Capitalism "cannot exist without constantly revolutionizing the means of production" and then everything else. As capital is made more efficient, it is accumulated into the hands of the most productive and the workers receive less, so their conditions grow continually worse. In response, they join trade unions that organize them and reach for power. "Now and again the workers are victorious," but it takes a shift of a "small section of the ruling class" and "a portion of the bourgeois ideologists" to create a critical mass for revolution. Only the conservative small businessmen and their

supporters and the "social scum" lowest classes resist, but the majority ultimately prevails. Private property is ended and all people become equal. While
Marx and Engels do not shrink from violence if it is required, they generally
expect that democracy could overthrow capitalism peacefully because the
masses desire equality and will support it politically if free to do so.

Marx argues that his new republic is not based upon subjective values but
is the conclusion demanded by a cold, rational scientific analysis. As proof,
his more intelligent followers point to the fact that most of his 10 policy proposals of 150 years ago have been adopted politically—not in so-called communist states—but in Europe and, to a good degree, in the U.S. where socialism was supposedly rejected. That is why his predictions cannot be dismissed
lightly. Highly progressive income taxes, centralization of credit in national
banks, communication and transportation centrally regulated by the state, a
common agricultural plan, comprehensive town planning and land use policies, and mandatory state education for all children—all of these proposals by
him have been adopted widely in modern democracies. Gradually, all unreg-
ulated capitalism will wear away and truly private property will disappear,
but enough wealth will have been created by then so that social needs can be
met under the final stage—socialism—without the hard work and struggles of
past ages. In the new brotherly world order, one can be a poet, lover, tinkerer,
and philosopher as one chooses and concentrate upon having fun.

This analysis and the recommendations based upon it were so powerful
that the whole history of the 20th century was dominated either by communist parties or by democratic socialist ones that adopted great parts of the
Marxian scientific plan. Its success can be measured by the fact that every
modern country—the others have to go through capitalism first—has adopted
a major part of the Marxian program and accepted its general goal of escap-
ing capitalist laws shielding property and its moral rules promoting hard work
and moral probity. Moreover, the collapse of the Soviet Union does not necessarily mean communism is done. Marx predicted success would be "by de-
grees." Perhaps it is still going forward but this time in the most developed
countries, where Marx actually predicted it would come and where his proposals have advanced so far, not in backward Russia.

It is of interest that not only have many of these "communist" policies
been implemented in many ways but many are similar to the proposals of
Plato in *The Republic*—abolition of private property, equal communal
sharing, state rearing of children, and the end of the traditional family. Do
science and reason both come to the same conclusion that these reforms are
required for commercial republics like Athens or the United States to become just societies?

WHO NEEDS VALUES?

As influential as Marx was, not all modern philosophical and scientific thought followed his in every regard. Most agreed with Marx that value was not transcendent nor metaphysical nor holy in the ancient or medieval senses. But the great philosopher Frederick Nietzsche found Marx's "classes" too abstract and not the essential social unit, which he claimed was "man," the individual. Following Descartes, he claimed that at bottom the only known value is the individual, but Descartes did not really strip away all tradition. Descartes accepted God, even Christian tradition, at least nominally. Nietzsche proclaimed the "death of god." Where is he? Where is the proof? In fact, there is nothing but individual men and women, Nietzsche said, who may or may not be captured by social institutions. The super man can face the hard reality and throw off all the shaping by society, all institutions, all myths, all external values, all comforting traditions, all cultural lies, and even all class restrictions.

Man is alone, without god or his rules or his governments, explains Nietzsche. Man exists to express himself. He is a "free spirit" who transvalues all values in himself, the only measure of everything. Even the value of pity, or mercy, is only manipulated by formal religion and society, especially in Christianity, as a way to trap and control the creativity of the superior person. The Nietzschean super man or woman becomes the model for the free, creative, uninhibited, individualistic spirit of modern man, as well as for the iron leaders required for the radical changes he demanded be enacted to root out the existing powers and the societal inhibitions they support.[12]

But scientific inquiry did not end even there. The great biologist, Charles Darwin, reported that science observed no Nietzschean "spirit"—although Nietzsche conceived this in material terms and also supported Darwin's "law of natural selection"—nor did it ascertain a Marxian class-man, but science only discovered an evolved animal that we call man. He has traditions and "values," but these simply are the attributes of an advanced animal evolved along social lines from lower level animals, with time and environment the only other influences. Animals are neither metaphysical nor holy nor do they have souls. Animals simply evolve and adapt to natural conditions. Biology is the science of man, the animal. Study biology and one can understand and enrich the life of humanity.[13]

A more empirical philosophy called positivism, tried to reconcile these two by conceding that there is both sense and value, but the later would better be called non-sense, in both of its meanings. Only material sense is worth studying, said A. J. Ayer (together with Marx, Nietzsche, and Darwin) but, going further, concluded that even logic has no sense-standing. Logic is only an "analytic," useful only to the extent that it assists in studying sense. Contrary to Aristotle (or even Descartes), there are no firm first principles. By itself, even the formal and informal language that composes logic is artificial and has no inherent meaning. All traditions and values clearly are non-sense, neither true nor false, as only sense data are real, with real meaning.[14] Sigmund Freud took this one step further by adding the mind to the material world, holding that sense data include psychological reality too. Seemingly spiritual things like dreams are material manifestations of a material mind. Human tradition is unique because humans can study, interpret, and reform behavior through self-knowledge. Man is an animal, but a different type whose mind is the critical element for study. The individual has meaning, not in a metaphysical sense, but in the fact that there is a whole individual sexual personality (ego) that makes a person a person. He and his culture are in no sense supermen, however, but beasts driven by neuroses. The mind, the supposed very instrument of reason itself, is led by sexual urges and anxieties—which are the essential facts of human nature.[15]

The end of the long modern subjection of tradition to radical questioning rests in "postmodernism." In this philosophical view, even facts are not true into themselves but have meaning only within the whole environmental circumstances, the "historical context." Contrary to Freud, there is not even the "fact" of sex. As the postmodern team of Kristine M. Baber and Colleen I. Murray put it: "A keystone of a postmodern perspective is the rejection of a unitary truth or knowledge." Individuals or students create their own meaning. All knowledge claims of tradition, philosophy, and science are "partial, fragmented and incomplete." They "reject the claim of modernists that only rational, abstract thought and scientific methodology can lead to valid knowledge." Sex, especially, is variable rather than the basic fact of human biology assumed by both tradition and science. The only guide is individual meaning—one's own "life stories"—one's own individual interpretations—interacting with the teachers' "authority" to explore all possibilities without any moral or logical limits whatsoever.[16]

OR, MAYBE, WE DO?

The general effect of this long attempt to rationalize values and make them scientific has been to question why people should support their traditions and its values. The result of this long search has been to weaken all traditions. By the beginning of the 21st century, not only was tradition per se shorn of any truth value by science and rationalism but language, family, social life, government, personality, sanity, sexual identity, fact, and even logic and science themselves were all rendered problematical—nothing means more than what anyone thinks.

This history suggests that man and woman are neurotic animals needing super leaders (or teachers) or powerful states or super individuals to control or inspire better material conditions. Yet, there is some lingering desire for the old values. Materialistic communism did fall and the Soviet Union ceased to exist in 1991, under assault from old, unscientific values like freedom, national tradition, economic prosperity, justice, and even religion. Even those postmodernists most alienated from traditional mores like Baber-Murray feel they must explain that they reject "total relativism," by opposing adult sex with children, for example, although without giving any good reason why if they are correct that all sex roles are arbitrary. Only Plato and Nietzsche do not blink at voiding all traditional values—and, maybe, not even Plato if he supported Socrates' decision to die for his tradition rather than escape his city's punishment. So only Nietzsche is left rejecting any value beyond the individual self whatsoever. Could he be a majority of one, the only one to get the world and Western civilization right?

NOTES

1. Plato, "The Allegory of the Cave," in *The Republic*, trans. Benjamin Jowlett (New York: Schribner, 1871).

2. Plato, *Meno*, trans. Benjamin Jowlett (New York: Schribner, 1871).

3. Leonard K. Nash, *The Nature of the Natural Sciences* (Boston: Little Brown, 1963).

4. Plato, *Crito*, trans. Benjamin Jowlett (Oxford: Clarendon, 1868).

5. Plato, *The Republic*, Book V.

6. Aristotle, "Posterior Analytics," in *Organon*, trans. G. R. G. Mure (Oxford: Clarendon, 1925), I: 1–3.

7. John Emerich Edward Dalberg-Acton, *Essays in the History of Liberty* (Indianapolis: Liberty Classics, 1986) I: 2 and 33; F. A. Hayek, *The Constitution of Liberty* (Chicago: University of Chicago Press, 1960), chap. 11.

8. R. Descartes, "Principal Rules of the Method," in *Discourse on Method*, trans. John Veitch (Edinburgh: Sutherland & Knox, 1853), II.

9. Francis Bacon, "Preface," in *The New Organon* (London: Pickering, 1850).

10. Jacques Barzun, *From Dawn to Decadence* (New York: Harper-Collins, 2000).

11. Karl Marx and Frederich Engels, *The Communist Manifesto*, trans. Samuel Moore with F. Engels (Chicago: Kerr, 1913). On Marx and fun, see Karl Marx, *Early Writings*, trans. T. B. Bottomore (London: Watts, 1963).

12. Frederich Nietzsche, *The Anti-Christ*, trans. H. L. Mencken (New York: Knopf, 1920), 4–7, 13, 15, and 18.

13. Charles Darwin, *The Decent of Man and Selection in Relation to Sex* (London: Murray, 1871).

14. A. J. Ayer, "The Function of Philosophy," in *Language, Truth and Logic* (New York: Dover, 1952), 46–50.

15. Sigmund Freud, "Psychoanalysis," in *An Outline of Psycho-Analysis*, trans. James Strachey (New York: Norton, 1949).

16. Kristine M. Baber and Colleen I. Murray, "A Postmodern Feminist Approach," *Family Relations*, (January 2000), 23–33.

Chapter Three

The Western Vision

WHAT IS THE WESTERN TRADITION?

Is It Greek?

Explaining Western civilization is not an easy or obvious task. And description must preceed analysis. While it is reasonably clear that the Western tradition is different from the other great traditions, it is not clear how it is so or how to define it or what makes it unique. What can be presumed is that the West has some set of values and institutions, whatever they are. In other words, it has a tradition or culture. While the thrust of the rationalist-scientific enterprise has been to question tradition—not only specific traditions, and especially the Western one, but also the whole idea of tradition itself—this assumed that there was a Western tradition that has values that needed to be questioned.

What is the tradition of the West, especially as it has been transferred to America, the ultimate object of our study? The most popular answer is that Western culture comes from Greece, especially from its major city Athens. So, is Western tradition Greek? Even if it is, it is not so clear what about Greek thought or history is critical. For example, classical scholars Victor Davis Hansen and John Heath say that what Athens contributed to Western civilization was its characteristic element, rationality, the rational-scientific way of thinking explored in the previous chapter.[1] The ancient historian Thucydides, however, quotes the great Athenian leader Pericles as saying its greatness came from the real historical experiences of the Athenian people and the democratic institutions they created (although Thucydides spends much of the rest of his book suggesting they were not so true to those principles after becoming powerful).[2] So, is the Western tradition reason or the

traditional institutions? Plato, in the *Crito*, told a story of an even darker
Athens that would kill its finest rational person in the name of its tradition.[3]
The third possibility is that it is Athens' cultic intolerance and closed-minded
piety drawn from the mists of time that has become the identifying characteristic of the Western tradition.

Socrates presents an interesting case. He rejected his friend Crito's advice
to escape after Athens' democratic leaders sentenced him to death for teaching "subversive" ideas to the young. Instead, Socrates insisted upon honoring
the city's traditions even though he thought they were wrong. He allowed tradition to trump the demands of rationalistic justice by allowing it to kill him.
On the other hand, given the fact that Socrates' nobility has survived to this
day and Athens' institutions have not, one could argue that reason ultimately
triumphed. Did Socrates honor both traditional and rationalistic elements by
his death? Importantly, Socrates wrote nothing about this himself but only
lived it. Socrates' dual loyalty was not explored initially, and the one who did
write about it, Plato, probably sympathized with Crito that he should not have
submitted to the tradition.

It is not until Aristotle, in his *Politics*, that this "dualistic" blend of virtues,
a middle way, is fully developed. In his values and in his methodology, both
traditional and rational elements pervade Aristotle's philosophy.[4] Yet, even
with Aristotle, it is difficult to argue that Western culture was actually established in Greece. Whatever Aristotle may have taught Alexander, the later in-
stituted absolute monarchy rather than the balanced polity his teacher favored. Aristotle's preferred form was not achieved in his time—nor for ages
thereafter. Even if one accepts Pericles' claim that the balanced republic was
a reality in Athens, it did not last long.

OR IS IT FROM JERUSALEM?

Israel is another civilization with deep roots that has a claim to being the
source of Western civilization. Both view the world as ordered and neither ir-
rationally capricious nor intractable. It is difficult to conceive of Western civilization without its concept of linear time nor its ideas of a created order and
justice. The Jews knew these things because their Creator told them, because
they were his favored people. Even time and history came from God and was
to be used effectively to follow his will toward his justice. While their nation
was favored, it was not guaranteed prosperity or order unless it fully followed
His law. He gave this moral law to control His people's passions and even
obliged them to love their neighbor. When they did not obey, retribution was
taken upon them but they could always return to him by following his path to

justice. A great part of Western energy undoubtedly arises from its impatience to use the time available to get good things accomplished. "You only go around once" is its secular rendition. The predominant Christian religion of the West certainly gets its moral values from Judaism, which its founder said he came to change not one iota. Even its idea that the world is rational enough that it can be studied and controlled can be traced to Judaism's idea of the ordered universe created by God. Are these ideas the essence of what is the West?[5]

OR FROM ROME?

Neither Greece nor Israel survived Rome. Indeed, it conquered and annihilated both Athens and Jerusalem. As the only civilization in the heartland of the West for almost a millennium, Rome obviously influenced its later history and is an obvious candidate to define its central values. According to one authority, the Roman contributions to the Western tradition can be summarized as: (1) a strong-stable civilization based upon law; (2) a practical bent in reasoning (Cicero or Seneca, as opposed to Plato); (3) the importance of the "public thing" (republic) rather than the merely private; (4) the ideal of the stoic, republican statesman as heroic leader especially in time of crisis; (5) the necessity of a strong magistrate and a bicameral legislature (with a strong Senate); and (6) a republican imagery, especially in architecture and institutions.[6] Yet, this very same authority argues that, while these six attributes did influence it, the West does not arise, except sporadically, until after Rome falls, in Europe. In any event, many of these ideals eroded early, beginning at the time of Julius Caesar. After a long degeneration of its prized rule of law, it declined from a republic into authoritarianism, and Rome likewise fell.

IS IT CHRISTENDOM?

The historic but now unfashionable argument has been that it was Christendom that made the West. Modern author Robert Royal summarizes the major influences of Christianity in creating the West as: (1) its roots in Judaism, whose ideas of Creator, nature, and time it added to its own and further fused into this the traditions of the European cults; (2) its "missionary fervor" that led its churches and monasteries to tame the disorder and darkness, whose peace was to last 1,000 years until Protestant-Catholic conflict undermined it; (3) its separation of church and state as a means to balance power and preserve the independence of the church; (4) its new morality for society, as taught by St. Augustine, that was wary of the state but also supported it; (5) its development of representative governmental institutions of lord (representing a geographical locality), bishop (representing the church), commoner (representing property), and king (representing the state); (6) its global perspective that moved it to reach out to and interact with every other culture; (7) its universal morality—citing de Vitoria's early doctrine on the moral equality of the Indians—represented by a "universal" church; (8) its universal appeal to different cultures, best expressed by the fact that its God sacrificed himself for man rather than vice versa, as in many cults; and (9) despite "occasional atrocities," it has had a "providential" role in leading the world to progress and prosperity.[7]

OR IS IT A MEDIEVAL SYNTHESIS?

Philosopher John Courtney Murray argues that it was not until the highpoint of Christian influence that the West, as such, was created during the Medieval period. It is especially the medieval idea of synthesis that is the essence of Western culture and thought, he claims.[8] The West is a synthesis of the Judaic history of God and creation and the Aristotelian philosophy of reason plus Christian salvation, revelation, and faith, as adopted within European history, institutions, and science. This synthetic vision was developed by and is summarized in the philosophy of St. Thomas Aquinas. This philosophy "did not start with God but merely with experience," indeed with the insights of a pagan philosopher, Aristotle, and so was not simply a myth of an historic people. Neither was it a simply abstract philosophy like Plato's or Descartes but started with the sense experience of the Western peoples. Indeed, Medieval Christianity added the belief that reason, science, faith, and tradition could not be in conflict with each other in the long run. "Between the valid conclusions of rational thought and the doctrines of faith, no unresolvable clash could or should occur." All were compatible with truth, if each honestly sought that truth.

The "betrayal' came when modern rationalism claimed, "there is only one form of rational truth." Contrary to modern philosophers, neither reason nor science logically leads to atheism, since God cannot be disproved by either method. Even if he did not exist, their methods could never discover this. Modern atheism, therefore, "is never a conclusion to a theory, philosophical or scientific. It is a decision, a free act of choice that antedates all theories," what Aristotle would call an assumption or axiom. All of these assumptions are of two kinds—pantheist monism and materialist monism—accepting only nature or only materialism as reality, both rejecting synthesis for either-or.

Both are first premises, or prejudices, not arguments. In fact, they reduce to only one first principle, monism—that there is only one way. Western thought is unique in being dualistic, accepting many possible explanations and rejecting none out of hand. This mode of thinking arises first in Aristotle but does not reach its developed form until medieval Europe where it became the basis for its science, its culture, and its institutions.

OR IS IT SIMPLY BRITISH?

Actually, we are searching for the Western tradition as it has particularly influenced the United States. Since America was a British colony for a century and a half before it became a separate nation, it is obvious that the manner in which Western tradition influenced Britain must have been imported to some degree across the ocean to the new world. The significant fact, according to the great historian Lord Acton was that Britain retained more of the medieval culture and institutions longer than any other European nation.[9] Because it was more isolated from later continental innovations in government and society that slowly eroded these feudal values in the face of a rising nationalism in the rest of Europe, Britain retained these values long enough to transfer them to America.

Consequently, one modern authority on the contribution of the British tradition to America stresses how it differs from the rest of Europe: (1) America's preference for British cultural conservatism over French radicalism; (2) America's common law–evolved legal system based upon English law rather than continental law derived from abstract principles; (3) America's reliance upon religion and church "as pillars of the social order" as in Britain, rather than antagonism with religion; (4) America's British practicality, even in religion; (5) the idea of both that their nations were divinely favored; (6) America's moderate British individualism (especially in the South); (7) mixed with community (especially in New England); (8) the positive view of both nations as business civilizations; (9) America's reliance upon the English language; and (10) its use of English literature (especially the King James version of the Bible and Shakespeare) as the basis for its own heritage.[10]

IS IT ALL OF THEM?

It seems reasonable to conclude that it was the merging of Greek rational freedom and Hebrew created order as filtered through Roman institutions on the ground culminating in Medieval Christian Europe, especially as it took form in early 17th century Britain, which created the Western civilization that was transferred to the United States. It was a combination of the history, institutions, and ideas of these different civilizations. It began with the rise of the ancient traditional codes of the Greek city states and persisted until the defeat of Athens by Philip II of Macedon in 338 B.C. and the parallel history of Abraham, Isaac, Jacob, and Moses and the life of Judaism under the Judges, Kings, the Captivity, the Return until the fall of Jerusalem in 70 A.D. Both of these developments clashed with the rise of another cult of the city in Rome and its codes of law, citizenship, republic, and empire, until its conversion to Christianity and its fall in A.D. 476. The arrival of a unique Christian civilization began with Constantine's toleration Edict of Milan in 313 and lasted until the Pope proclaimed Charlemagne king in 773. The Medieval period can be dated from Charlemagne's Carolingian dynasty, through the Normans and the crusades, to the Aquinas institutionalization of Aristotle, until this consensus was challenged by Martin Luther in 1513. While the British tradition had ancient roots, it cohered with the conversion of the Celts in the early fifth century to Christianity and flowered under a local-based and complex social order, a Magna Charta and rights of Englishmen that made even the king subject to the law, and parliaments that represented the people and the interests of the nation in governing it—ideas that were brought to America during its colonial period.

Importantly, this conclusion that the West is a combination of these traditions can be supported coming from either the conservative or progressive points of view. The modern conservative philosopher Frank Meyer directly made the case that this synthesis of civilizational values and institutions constituted the Western tradition.[11] While Michael Walzer—a leading figure of the political left in the United States—did not specify this specific set of traditions as the essential values, he did make the idea of synthesis the defining ideal of the American social order. Critically, it was the progressive who made the telling observation that there was something about the oneness of ancient Greek society and thought—and all others—that made them less than fully Western.[12]

It will be argued here, therefore, that in some way or another, it was the idea of synthesis of ideas and institutions that was unique about and describes the Western tradition—ideas and institutions in "high tension," as Meyer put it. The West epitomizes this idea of "dualism"—or of using two or more ideas or things in tension, of synthesis, of (rough) harmony, of (tenuous) balance—as a unique Western way of viewing values, institutions, and all reality. As the rationalists Descartes, Bacon, Nietzsche, etc. make evident, these authors would simply consider this "sloppy thinking." Reason is unitary, they argue, and leads in one direction—deductively or inductively—toward truth. Obviously, this is at the highest-level of disagreement conceivable—monism or dualism are first principles or axioms—and cannot be satisfactorily resolved here. Regardless, dualism as a way of thinking begins in Aristotle and runs through Rome, up to St. Thomas and the Middle Ages, and through all European history—but especially England's—to the United States and will be the main focus henceforth.

In modern times, it is the philosopher of science Sir Karl Popper, who makes the argument that—contrary to the rationalists—there is no single, unitary method that constitutes science or reason. Each one of the great philosophers or scientists considered in the previous chapter discovered a new means to understand reality and claimed that it, alone, was the way to truth. All of them provided some insight, but only some; none encompassed all knowledge. It was not strange that Descartes or any of the others found uncertainty in medieval Aristotelian science—with Aristotle partially responsible because he promised more certainty than is possible to deliver, as did Bacon more extensively and more rashly. For even the most modern science can be mistaken in its conclusions, like any thinking, and results since Pascal are probable rather than absolute in any event. Science, in fact, is only reasoning generally, Popper claims. If there is "one" method, it is simply "critical thinking."

Critical thinking can use both empirical and analytical approaches depending upon the problem to be investigated. In this sense, it is dualistic. True science even has an element of tradition. The search for truth that underlies all science is a metaphysical assumption grounded in tradition, but one that is needed if science itself is to make any sense at all. "All science is cosmology," Popper argues, and indeed in all science "metaphysical ideas have shown the way." The whole scientific enterprise depends upon metaphysical assumptions such as believing there is enough order in the universe that allows it to be studied profitably, derived from the Judaic presumption that there is an ordered universe. Values, thus, rest at the heart of science too and must be used as a starting point. Science and reason must start with and simplify traditional common sense to understand the more complex underlying reality—as Aristotle maintained—and in that sense they both depend upon humble tradition to begin. So, tradition and its values cannot be dismissed by science or rationalism because both depend upon it themselves.[13]

When science tries to act in a single-minded way to describe all reality, it stretches it to irrelevance. Descartes' analytical geometry is useful for spatial thinking but no one yet has made his physics empirically meaningful. Bacon's inductive method is useful in testing but no one has been able to use it to build up systematically to a higher physical truth (as Aristotle predicted could not be done). Plato's questioning becomes sophistic without right reason. Ruthless questioning can reveal some insights, but as theologian and mystery novelist Dorothy Sayers noted, rationalistic method can lead to absurdity when using methods inappropriate to the problem investigated. She poked fun by performing a Biblical-type exegesis on Sherlock Holmes' Dr. Watson to find evidence about him that was not given by author Arthur C. Doyle.[14] Of course, it is difficult to know oneself, much less a figure remote in time, and of course there is no "additional" information about a fictional character—so the results are meaningless. The more modern explanation is, garbage in, garbage out.

Political scientist Alfred deGrazia makes the point that there is a difference between scientific truth and what the scientific establishment says it is. In a famous study, he compared how the actual scientific establishment in the U.S. treated the findings of Dr. Immanuel Velikovsky in the 1960s compared to how its own rational "reception system" says he should have been treated. DeGrazia's research found that the scientific community acted more like a tradition than a science. It rejected Velikovsky's evidence, often without even reading it, and certainly did not make a reasoned criticism. They were, however, able to dismiss him successfully as a charlatan. Forty years later, in terms of many of the specifics of the debate—the temperature of Venus, the movement of the continents, the effects of sun spots, and the role of crisis events relative to evolution—Velikovsky seems more correct today than his critics, but he still is considered a crank, partially because much of science is still looking for a single solution.[15]

Nobel Laureate F. A. Hayek argued that today there are two philosophical tendencies within the overall tradition of Western rationalism, what the medievalists would call the monists and the dualists. Hayek labeled the first, constructive rationalism. It considers all true thinking as rationally deductive only, that all inconsistencies can be resolved by logic and testing alone. Society is a deliberate, rational creation where all social consequences follow from one guiding ideal. Every particular case can be resolved from the logic of the abstract plan. The model is Plato's Republic ordered under the single standard of justice for all or Rousseau's society based solely upon reason, where a strong government can plan rationally for society. The vision is French, with a notable exception being Bacon. The second, critical rationalism, is not simply rational but is deductive, empirical, intuitive, and traditional. Society is evolutionary, a spontaneous order where general rules only broadly steer behavior rather than directly produce solutions. Individual cases are settled on various traditional moral rules that cannot be deduced from abstract rules. The model is Aristotle's mixed polity, Thomas Aquinas' complex medieval society, and the mixed constitution of John Locke. The viewpoint is more British, with a notable exception being Alexis de Tocqueville.

Hayek claimed that constructive rationalism did seek rationality univocally, in a single-minded search for truth, starting in the modern period with

Descartes. Critical rationalism balanced rationality and empiricism, balanced the abstract and intuitive, balanced order and creativity, balanced rules and liberty, balanced state and church, balanced property and obligation. It was critical rationalism—incorporating Greek, Jewish, Roman, Christian, and Medieval perspectives—that had the greatest influence upon the British thinking that was transferred to America during its colonial period.[16]

JOHN LOCKE AND THE WESTERN VISION

It is the great English political philosopher, John Locke, who most clearly connects the medieval, critical rationalist means of thinking to America. He is almost universally accepted as the major inspiration for its social and political beliefs. Historian Louis Hartz claimed the connection was so close that "history was on a lark" to bind Locke's thought to American practice.[17] Locke explicitly related his thinking to the medieval philosophers Hooker, Grotius, and Pufendorf, who were late students of Aquinas, who adapted Aristotle. Locke contrasted his treatise commonwealth to the constructivist republics created by more contemporary philosophers like Hobbes and Filmer, who were more influenced by Plato. Society, Locke argued, did rise from freedom in nature, as the others claimed; yet, nature was not fully free but had its controls. There was a natural liberty in the state of nature for mere self-preservation, but both reason and the fact that all were created equally by God—who commanded all to follow His law—required all to preserve others too, especially one's family and neighbors. It was not a Hobbesian war of all against all because God positively required man not to harm his neighbor, at least if he did not first injure him and respected his property. While some broke God's law, enough initially followed it or were dissuaded by the rough equality of power and property in the state of nature that there was relative peace.

As population grew, however, increasingly complex property relationships raised many issues that needed to be settled between neighbors. Property became "very unsafe, very insecure" in the state of nature so men freely consented to give up "all the power necessary" to secure peace to a government. They would not give up all power but only that necessary to protect property, life, and freedom. It would have been irrational to give unlimited power to a ruler, and God did not require this. That power would be limited because the government would follow "an established, settled, known law, received and allowed by common consent to be the standard of right and wrong and the common measure to decide all controversies." If that law were to be applied fairly to all, they also needed "a known and indifferent judge with the authority to determine all differences according to the established law." Power would be limited further by dividing it between a legislative assembly that set the rules and a separate executive that would carry them out. As long as these did not exceed the power granted to them, the people must follow the law or suffer the consequences. Since the law was to be derived from traditional, "settled" beliefs, most will in fact follow the law naturally. Within the rules, there is significant freedom to live much like one did in the state of nature. If the authorities abuse the people's rights, the people can "appeal to heaven" and revolt, although only in serious cases will this right be exercised.[18]

The Western vision as it was transferred to America through John Locke was a synthesis of values developed historically and rooted in English practice. In this, it followed Aristotle rather than Plato, St. Thomas rather than Descartes. It was not a monist or unitary vision, not a comprehensive, abstract, constructivist design. It was neither a Platonic ideal republic nor a Marxist scientific utopia. It was developed evolutionarily, historically, empirically—with rational elements but also with traditional and even theological ones, specifically Judeo-Christian ones. Locke taught both reason and tradition, natural law and God's law, state and society, popular consent and government power, law and settled beliefs, executive and legislative, individual freedom and community responsibility, property and family obligation, a right to revolution but a reluctance to invoke it. All was division, balance, and harmony.[19]

The contract between individual, community, and state was sealed upon the basis of common consent. All were protected by dividing power between executive and legislature, and independent and neutral courts. Consent was so important that revolution was justified if the state broke the contract. Within the rules, consent implied great freedom, which relied upon virtue and obligation in the people to keep social order rather than upon concentrated state power. These Lockean views—especially that sovereignty can be efficiently divided—have been called outright irrational and having it both ways by constructivists—even as they have had difficulty excluding Locke from the pantheon of philosophers. One critic simply excluded half of Locke's philosophy to allow him to qualify on rational grounds alone.[20] Whether rational or not, this Lockean way of thinking was transferred to America, where it was received as its early vision for both its society and its government.

NOTES

1. Victor Davis Hanson and and John Heath, *Who Killed Homer?* (New York: Free Press, 1998).

2. Thucydides, "Pericles' Funeral Oration," in *The History of the Peloponnesian War*, trans. Richard Crowley (London: Longmans, Green, 1876).

3. Plato, *Crito*, trans. Benjamin Jowlett (Oxford: Clarendon, 1868).

4. Aristotle, "The Character of Citizens," in *The Politics*, trans. William Ellis (London: Dent & Sons, 1912), VII, 7.

5. Herbert Butterfield, "Originality of the Old Testament," in C. Thomas McIntire, ed., *Writings on Christianity and History* (New York: Oxford University Press, 1979)and Paul Johnson, *A History of the Jews* (New York: Harper & Row, 1987).

6. Michael Lind, "The Second Fall of Rome," *The Wilson Quarterly* (Winter 2000).

7. Robert Royal, "Who Put the West in Western Civilization?" in *The Intercollegiate Review* (Spring 1998).

8. J. C. Murray, "Medieval Synthesis," in *Death of God* (New Haven: Yale University Press, 1942), 3 and 87–95, The Medieval synthesis differed from Marxian or Hagelian synthesis in two major ways. The latter's synthesis was a result of the interaction between two prior forces (called thesis and antithesis) where the two prior forces collided and disappeared into a third force, the synthesis. Medieval synthesis preserved the separate forces that remained in continuing tension with each other. Second, the Marxian-Hagelian synthesis was developmental over time while the medieval thesis could change or remain in constant tension. The Marxian synthesis also was materialistic only.

9. John Emerich Edward Dalberg-Acton, *Essays in the History of Liberty* (Indianapolis: Liberty Classics, 1986), 52–53.

10. Louis Wright, "The British Tradition in America in Retrospect," in *Tradition and the Founding Fathers* (Charlottesville, Va.: Thomas Jefferson Memorial Foundation, 1975).

11. Frank Meyer, "Western Civilization," *Modern Age* (Spring 1968).

12. Michael Walzer, "The Idea of Civil Society" *Dissent* (Spring 1991).

13. Karl Popper, "Preface 1958," in *The Logic of Scientific Discovery* (New York: Harper & Row, 1965).

14. Dorothy Sayers, "Dates in the Red-Headed League," in *Whimsical Christian* (New York: Scribner, 1978).

15. Alfred deGrazia, "The Scientific Reception System," in *The Velikofsky Affair* (New Hyde Park, N.Y.: University Books, 1966).

16. F. A. Hayek, "Kinds of Rationalism," in *Studies in Philosophy, Politics and Economics* (Chicago: University of Chicago Press), chap. 5.

17. Louis Hartz, *The Liberal Tradition in America* (New York: Harcourt, Brace, World, 1955; Devine, *The Political Culture of the United States*, 46–50.

18. John Locke, *Second Treatise on Government*, in Ernest Barker, ed., *Social Contract* (New York: Oxford University Press, 1962).

19. Donald J. Devine, *Does Freedom Work?* (Ottawa, Ill.: Caroline House, 1978), chap. 1.

20. Donald J. Devine, "John Locke: His Harmony Between Liberty and Virtue," *Modern Age* (Summer 1968), 246–56.

Chapter Four

American Values and Institutions

WHAT ARE AMERICAN VALUES?

What is America's unique vision? Almost a century and a half of colonial living preceded the Constitution and the new union that followed from it. Consequently, its culture had a long time to nourish at its English roots. Yet, the British values also were modified in the process by the fact that the colonies were separated from the mother country by a large ocean with slow means of communications between them. Like most cultures, the American one began in isolation with its own tradition. To assess the nature of the values that were actually transferred to the new nation, it is necessary to begin with the settlement period.

The first British colony, Virginia, was chartered as a government-supported corporation under James I, the son of the beheaded Mary Queen of Scots (but ally of her opponent, Elizabeth), and was settled by English colonists in 1607. Jamestown almost did not survive, and when it was rescued, the government was granted quasi-dictatorial powers, not unusual for the times, as a means to revive it. A local assembly was allowed in 1619, although following the practice in the old country, it was originally dominated by a few wealthy planters and merchants. At the beginning, Virginia was pretty much a replica of the historical English society, medieval-based but Protestant and episcopal and built upon king and parliament. In the spirit of the times, the colony even had an Anglican established church supported by taxes that was united to the king and state but somewhat independent of them, as successive Episcopal, Puritan, and Catholic rulers guaranteed.[1]

ARE AMERICAN VALUES RELIGIOUS?

The Pilgrims who landed at Plymouth in 1620 to form the second colony were Puritans, a "dissenting" or "nonconformist" sect that rejected the established church as lax and corrupt. In spite of their dissent, they were able to win a charter to establish their religion in America. The Mayflower Compact, signed just before departing ship, had a decidedly religious tone but was also based upon majority rule and allegiance to the king. A second Puritan colony was founded as Massachusetts Bay a decade later and ultimately incorporated Plymouth. John Winthrop, one of the colony's great early leaders, expressed the values of the Puritan settlers best.[2] His message was Christian but he claimed there were "double laws," man's and God's. With Puritans, these overlapped to a great extent since God's law covered all of life and His was clearly the more important. Man's justice was important—especially to mollify the king, who allowed the nonconformity as long as it was well removed from England. But God's mercy clearly was the highest value to the dissenting colonists, and it was humanity's mission to take this Christian value to the world. This they did by establishing the Puritan church and governing their colonies in Massachusetts according to that law. From the beginning, there were disagreements regarding what God's law meant in public life, even among fellow non-conformists. So, banished for his different views and with the unsettled space available in this great wilderness, Roger Williams founded a new colony with more a liberal Christian interpretation, Rhode Island, in 1636.

The third colony was founded by a Catholic, Lord Baltimore, who established Maryland in 1632. It was unique in that its charter granted the franchise to all free men with no property qualifications. In 1649, it adopted a Toleration Act that Lord Acton called the basis for the first free society in the modern world.[3] All Christian religions were officially tolerated and Judaism was so in practice.[4] It was not a coincidence that Charles II had tried toleration in the Old World, for Acton traced the attitude of both to the medieval structure and values still existent in England more than elsewhere at this time—but which withered there as a result of events leading to the Royalist-Puritan wars. The Maryland Toleration Act was voided by Parliament in 1689 as too tolerant, especially of Catholics, and the idea died in America too. Yet, not ten years later it was revived in spirit by the Christian Quaker William Penn, in the American commonwealth still bearing his name.

Actually, the first settled town in what is now the U.S. was much earlier, in 1565, by the Spanish in Florida and was named after a religious figure, St. Augustine. Indeed, it was not Britain but colonial Spain, under the influence of a Catholic monk, which was the first to set the policy of treating Native

Americans as equal moral beings, although it often failed to be observed in practice. Religion was even more important to the French colonies, whose policy against immigration of Europeans forced them to rely upon and trade peacefully with the Indians. With few officials and little force or government to speak of, religious missionaries were critical to create the close relationships with the natives necessary to support their operations. So, wherever one looked in early America, religion was central to the values and institutions established there. But it was very diverse in form in the different colonies, and it produced very different results for each.

OR ARE AMERICAN VALUES PRACTICAL, SECULAR, COMMONSENSICAL?

As the population spread from the ports to the countryside, as different religious populations mixed, and as a more commercial perspective became more widespread, a certain practicality in public affairs became more common. Was this more practical common sense then the core of the values of these early Americans?

By the early 18th century, Benjamin Franklin's *Poor Richards Almanack* was by far the best-selling book after the Bible. At the time of the Revolution, it represented the practical, commonsensical, secular rather than religious, side of the American character. The Almanac was a litany of common sense prescriptions — work hard; save; early-to-bed; healthy, wealthy, and wise practical advice. While it relied upon many Biblical quotations, they were invoked for their practical utility rather than for religious inspiration. The purpose was secular success rather than religious edification, although the common symbolism undoubtedly added to its popularity. The practical almanac had great influence on the thought of the American colonies even though Franklin in his wise and witty way downplayed it, when he said people listened to Richard but "practiced the contrary!"[5] In fact, almost every American colonist could quote an aphorism or two from Franklin, even if they did not always follow them.

OR ARE THEY BOTH?

As with the Western tradition generally, we will argue that American values are based upon a synthesis of religious and practical traditions. This is best demonstrated in the document that affirmed the new American nation, the Declaration of Independence. This founding document demonstrated that both religious and practical values were central to the formation of the new nation. The Declaration first expressed explicit values based upon the old religious tradition: "We hold these truths to be self-evident, that all men are created equal, that they are endowed by their Creator with certain unalienable rights, that among these are life, liberty and the pursuit of happiness."[6] Creator, of course, was the Jewish concept for God the Father in the Christian creed. And life, liberty, and happiness summarized the values Locke said were granted by Him to all. If these rights were not respected by government, the people had a moral right to rebel. So, most of the rest of the Declaration was a practical spelling out of grievances that Americans held against the King in a commonsensical attempt to win over the "opinion of mankind" to the justness of their revolution. This founding document of the new nation makes it evident that both the religious and practical aspects of colonial America formed the basis of its dual argument for its very existence.

The Constitution explicitly followed in that tradition by seeing human nature not as a univocal theme but as a balance between angelic and troublesome tendencies, as documented in its justifying work called *The Federalist Papers*. According to the so-called "father of the Constitution" James Madison, differences, divisions, factions, and even conflict are innate to social life. They will arise naturally even from any minor disagreements. Major ones, like religion, have led to great disorder. But the most enduring source of conflict is over property. These differences in wealth and income, however, naturally arise from freedom. The only way to eliminate these and other differences, he argued in Federalist 10, would be for government to extinguish liberty or make people all think the same. Both require the improper and imprudent use of force by government. Eliminating liberty would be like eliminating air because it feeds fire and fire can be dangerous. Liberty is just as essential to healthy social life, even if it can be abused. Likewise, if people are free, it is impossible for all to have the same views. With all of the different sects in the new nation and with private property ownership spread so widely, enormous force would be required for a common national religion or for an equal distribution of wealth. Instead, freedom and private property must be protected as the "first object" of government. The only way to respect liberty and protect property and religious differences is to create an independent secular government that is limited in the powers that it can exercise over them.[7] In that way, both secular and religious freedom can be guaranteed.

WHAT IS THE AMERICAN GOVERNMENT?

The People?

If man were a devil, no good form of government could be created because he would have to corrupt it. If he were an angel, no government would be necessary to control him because he would always act virtuously, Madison continued in Federalist 51. But in a government of real people over real people, ambition must be made to check ambition by placing leaders into different power institutions that counteract each other's dangerous ambitions. The preeminent way to limit ambition is to have the people control the rulers through elections. A House of Representatives representing all of the citizens would be created to do so. Membership in this legislative body was to be open to all free male adults without any major qualification, although the states were allowed to set basic requirements and did. There were frequent elections every two years to keep representatives close to the people, districts were comparatively small to make them pay attention to local interests, and all laws were to apply to the legislators themselves so that they would pass fair laws in their own self-interest as well as that of the citizens. In short, it was essential to have the people rule through such a democratic institution. But experience demonstrated to the Founders that direct democracy by itself was not enough—history proved that no pure democracy had survived more than a few years. As Plato and Aristotle had warned, elected officials could appeal to people's selfish as well as angelic appetites and bring the system down.

THE INSTITUTIONS?

"A dependence upon the people is, no doubt, the primary control on the government," Madison added, "but experience has taught mankind the necessity of auxiliary precautions."[8] These further "precautions" were governmental institutions that were popularly based but also had some independence from popular passion to act on their own for the public good. The new government's national scope meant that the larger the geographical area covered, the less likely popular prejudice in one region could adversely affect the whole. But the major precaution to avoid tyranny was to divide power between different institutions—between state and national levels and among legislative, executive, and judicial national institutions.

The central underlying principle of the whole new government was this separation of powers. The new government would check and balance power between separate institutions as a means both for government action when required and for limiting power when not necessary. Ambition would check ambition in different power institutions so that no one institution— even the most democratic one—could dominate the rest and threaten liberty.

CHECKS AND BALANCES

The Constitution's job was primarily to define the institutions of this check-and-balance government. It was not primarily a statement granting rights—and the Bill of Rights was not passed until later—although some other rights were granted by the Constitution itself. The Constitution can be most easily defined by identifying its five main articles, each one of which established or recognized a different power-checking institution. Each of these—legislative, executive, judicial, states, and amendment process—had different powers that allowed it to carry out its function but each also had its own powers to check abuses by the others.

Article I made the legislature, Congress, composed of two houses, the first institution of the government. As noted, the people were given representation by voting for a House member elected directly by popular vote. A second house, the Senate, was elected indirectly, through the state legislatures—which were thought of as very democratic, being smaller and closer to the people. Because Congress was to represent the people themselves, it was granted the most power, to pass all laws, but both houses had to do so in complete agreement, each house balancing the other to prevent abuse. As Article I, Section 8, made clear, Congress was supposed to act only in seventeen or so well-defined circumstances and the division of power made it difficult to accomplish even these few. But the idea was that if most social activity was done outside national government by states and the people privately, the fewer, more important national political matters would be less likely to produce discord—so they could be resolved more easily. National powers were limited further by Section 9, which did not allow the executive to arrest a person without justifying it to a judge (the right of habeas corpus) except in emergencies, nor permit legislative actions to target specific persons rather than using general rules of law (a bill of attainder), nor pass a law after the fact to make something illegal that was not so when the act was performed (ex post facto laws), nor enact a direct, national (income) tax, or grant favoritism to any one state over another.

Article II created an executive power to rest in one person, a president. A vice president simply stood ready to take his place upon death. The president was to supply the energy to the new government and was commander-in-chief of the military. He was not directly elected by the people, but was elected by local notables, in an Electoral College that was steadily democratized over time by the political party system. The power of commander-in-chief and negotiating treaties and selecting ambassadors, with the consent of two-thirds of the Senate, made him preeminent in foreign affairs—although Congress was given the power to declare war and to decide how much—if any—money would be spent upon it. Domestically, the president was, formally, only to ask the opinions of the chief department officers in writing. But this implied more control over the bureaucracy since he appointed all officers — although even this was with the advice and consent of the Senate. Congress' power of the purse and its ability to legally limit executive flexibility forced divided loyalty from the bureaucracy, but the cabinet officers had the day-to-day authority and they were loyal to the president, which made him the most powerful single person in the government

Article III created a Supreme Court and such appellate courts as Congress authorized. Appointments, by the president with Senate advice and consent, were for life to give independence in their judicial decisions. Original jurisdiction was granted over the Constitution and disputes between the states, to which Congress could and did add appellate authority over the laws it passed. Every federal case and controversy would be settled by it, and its final say on cases would ultimately give it great control over policy by refusing to enforce laws that it deemed unconstitutional.

Article IV applied to the states, requiring that each give full faith and credit to each other's laws, respect the privileges and immunities of each other, and honor extradition for crimes committed in each other's state — including for escaped slaves, although the international slave trade was to be eliminated by 1808. Each state was guaranteed a republican form of government and protection against invasion or, when requested by the state, against domestic violence. Otherwise, states were left pretty much to their own resources, which at the beginning were collectively much greater than those of the national government.

Article V provided for amendment of the whole document. Amendments could be proposed by two-thirds of both houses of Congress or by two-thirds of the states, which could call for a Convention, in either case to propose additions to or changes in existing provisions. To be adopted as legally part of the Constitution, proposed changes had to be approved by three-fourths of the states. The only limit on amendments after 1808 was against denying equal representation of states in the Senate. Otherwise, any or every part of the original Constitution was subject to change.

WHAT ARE AMERICAN RIGHTS?

If checks and balances were to be the major protection of people's rights, what need was there for a Bill of Rights? Many of the Founders, in fact, did not believe one was necessary, and there was not one in the Constitution that was originally placed into effect by the states. But during the ratification debates some states passed resolutions requesting a bill of rights, as had long existed for all Englishmen in the mother country. Twelve separate amendments to the Constitution were proposed by the first Congress to become an American Bill of Rights. One amendment has not yet been adopted, and a second was not approved until 1992. So the remaining ten original proposals are today called the Bill of Rights and are listed as the first ten amendments. While many of the ten list rights for individuals, they were composed as restrictions upon the new national government's power, to allay fears that the new government would become as oppressive as the old king's.

The First Amendment specified that Congress could make no law establishing religion or limiting the free exercise thereof, or to limit freedom of press, speech, assembly, association, or petition. The second provided for a right to keep and bear arms. The third did not allow quartering of troops in people's homes. The fourth opposed unreasonable searches and seizures of individuals. The fifth required legal due process, indictments before trials, forbade multiple attempts at conviction for the same crime (double jeopardy), and protected private property. The sixth required a jury trial for criminal offenses, and the seventh for civil procedures. The eighth opposed excessive bail. The ninth specified that the enumeration of these rights did not imply that other rights were not protected. The tenth summarized that it was a government of limited powers by saying that the powers not delegated to the United States nor prohibited to the states by the Constitution were reserved to the states or to the people.

The amendments were both a statement of rights and a limit on national power, with the later the effective legal attribute at the beginning. Freedom of speech, press, religion, assembly, and property were originally guaranteed against the national government only.[10] Several states even had established religions at the time the rights were adopted. So, the Bill of Rights originally did not apply to state government actions, although each state had its own bill of rights or similar protections for rights in their own laws. Nor were the Federal rights thought of even for the national government in absolute terms. For example, nine years later the Congress adopted the Alien and Sedition Acts to stop newspapers from publishing or discussing information about the government that could be harmful to its security, which its critics were unsuccessful in decrying as legal violations of freedom of speech and press.

While the rights that the Bill of Rights recognized were extremely important to early Americans, it should also be reiterated that certain other traditional "rights of Englishmen" were included in the Constitution itself. Thus the rights of habeas corpus and against a bill of attainder and ex post fact laws were deemed so important they were placed in the original document. And abridging those rights was forbidden also to the states. It was not until later that the rights of the first amendments were seen as a positive means for the national government to limit local and state government (19th century) and private and corporate (20th century) power.

NATIONAL POWER OR LOCAL AND VOLUNTARY CONTROL?

With only a score of powers or so directly granted to the national government, how could the people obtain the things they needed for a decent social life? Before the new constitution, a French naturalized New Yorker, Hector St. John de Crevecoeur, found that the early Americans were generally prosperous "because each person works for himself," unlike Europe with its "aristocratical families" and great kingly courts. Its social harmony did not even result from a common set of beliefs on a broad array of public issues. While the main culture came from England, many nations had settled there—adding their own Scottish, Irish, Dutch, Swedish, and other traditions to the mix. Substantial regional and great religious differences existed too. Yet, these were much more moderate and less dangerous than in Europe and were handled relatively peaceably by the state and local governments. In general, these new Americans were very individualistic, self-supporting, diverse, and peaceable. The only unity was a "pleasant uniformity of decent competency."[11]

Four decades later, the French aristocrat Alexis de Tocqueville performed the most systematic and influential investigation of what made the new American democracy tick. When he looked for evidence of the effect of the new national government around the country, he found it quite absent. Almost everything was accomplished outside of national government, which primarily handled national defense and limited inter-state commerce matters. Yet, he concluded, while the institutions of central power were missing, the people carried the nation in their hearts. This, paradoxically, made Americans more patriotic than in Europe where national government was visible and present everywhere. The American government, being less intrusive in people's lives, could be loved that much more.

The only effective government de Tocqueville discovered in America was local government.[12] Indeed, the overwhelming amount of government activity was local until the early 20th century in the United States. Local government had much less expertise, he argued, but it was more effective because it was present, knew local circumstances, and everyone willingly chipped in with the needed work. Even more work was performed by voluntary associations, including religious ones—about which he was, unlike Crevecoeur, very positive.[13] Much more work was performed by associations and local government than was performed by state and national government combined, or even by private enterprise. To him, wide participation in formal and informal associations was democracy in action—direct civic action was much more important than was mere voting participation. With no hereditary nobility and a wide franchise, there was a certain equality between citizens that made them feel part of the community and willing to act voluntarily to support it.

It was not the national government, as in France, nor a socially-conscious aristocracy, as in Britain, that accomplished great works in America, de Tocqueville concluded. It was local people with the freedom to solve their own problems that encouraged them to act in the community—and act more effectively than national government or aristocracy could. At bottom, success came not from national greatness but rested upon the individual responsibility of every citizen to pitch in and do what was needed for the community. Paradoxically, this limited national power made the national government stronger, not weaker, in the hearts of its countrymen. The national government, doing little to help the citizens also did little to oppress them either and was free to receive the accolades for the success of the whole governmental system. He predicted the rest of the world would follow in the same direction, at least toward more democracy and more equality.

SO, WHO IS IN CHARGE?
WHAT IS THE SUPREME POWER IN THE UNITED STATES?

The legislature, as the representative of the people and creator of all law, might seem the center of power in the American Constitutional government. But with this great grant of power, two houses were created, one based upon democratic population and one based upon equal state representation so that this great power was dissipated. The Congress further had a balance of direct democratic representation in the House and indirect state and local democratic representation in the Senate, so that each was given a somewhat different base of popular power. To this was added a veto power for the President that could only be overridden by a two-thirds majority in each house, a very difficult consensus to achieve in a representative legislative body. With all of this division in internal power and an external veto, Congress is normally limited in what it can plan and accomplish.

So, is the President supreme? The veto is certainly a powerful weapon. Yet, it is a negative rather than a positive power. He cannot pass a law or act without Congressional authorization or at least forbearance. While presidents have acted on their own for what they proclaimed as emergency situations, this executive discretion was balanced by giving Congress the power to impeach him or withhold the funds for everything he wants to do. In addition, courts can overrule his decisions. Well, then, are judges made so independent with life terms and the ability to interpret laws and the Constitution that the Supreme Court is supreme? Does it not have the "supremacy clause" to support its claim to ultimate power? No, courts need the executive to enforce every ruling they issue, which presidents such as Andrew Jackson and Abraham Lincoln have sometimes refused to do—and Congress must grant appropriations for them to be able to hold trials and punish those convicted. Congress even has the power to decide what is the appellate jurisdiction for the Supreme Court, the vast majority of its current authority.

All of this is balanced by independent states, which were assumed to have the real democratic power of the people behind them because they were closer to them and trusted more. Clearly, it was the states that were the ones primarily bound by the new Constitution, but they were left significant independent power, whose limit is in debate up to the present day. Importantly, only the states can amend the whole Constitution by two-thirds vote and could then themselves ratify their own proposals by three-fourths vote. They could change the whole nature of the system without any participation from the other three branches, as they did to establish the Constitution in the first place.

The unique insight of the U.S. Constitution was to divide power and have no single, ultimate source for it. All of the institutions would check each other to restrain abuses by the other. This was so radical that Alexander Hamilton in Federalist 9 called it a "new science of politics"—the idea that a people could disperse power, over a large expanse of territory, into a divided legislature, an independent court, a restricted executive, and sovereign states and still have a successful government.[14] This was a new and very complex government to say the least, requiring vast cooperation if it was to work at all. The House, Senate, President, Supreme Court and subordinate courts, ultimately 50 "sovereign" states, and an amendment process that can change all of the rest—all of these need to agree or defer if anything was to work without being blocked by one or more of the others. How could anything ever get done?

No other government divides power so much, without one place where it ultimately resides. The Founders could only do so if they expected a certain amity between the branches and that most things would be done outside national government, by the people, or by the states, as the Federalist said and the 10th Amendment guaranteed. No one in his right mind would divide power into so many parts if the idea were for the government to be the major decision-maker and for it to act efficiently on a wide range of issues. Consequently, most experts—believing that power must rest in one central place for anything to be accomplished—thought that government must of necessity be the essential actor to direct social life. All of the rationalists of Europe predicted certain doom for this new government that could not even concentrate power sufficiently to achieve the grand goals necessary for it to become a great nation.

NOTES

1. Acton, *Essays in the History of Liberty*, Chaps. 2–6, 16–17.

2. John Winthrop, *A Model of Christian Charity* (Boston: Massachusetts Historical Society, 1838).

3. John Emerich Edward Dalberg-Acton, *Essays in the Study and Writing of History* (Indianapolis: Liberty Classics, 1986), chap. 7, especially 131.

4. Edward C. Papenfuse, Jr., "The Maryland Act of Toleration of 1649," remarks to the House and Senate of Maryland, 25 March 1999.

5. Benjamin Franklin, *The Way to Wealth* (London: Simmons and Kirkby, 1775).

6. *The Declaration of Independence* (Baltimore: Mary Katherine Goddard, 1777).

7. *The Federalist Papers* (New York: New American Library, 1961), No. 10.

8. *The Federalist Papers*, No. 51.

10. The Bill of Rights was passed by Congress on September 25, 1789, and ratified by three-fourths of the states on December 15, 1791.

11. Hector St. John de Crevecoeur, "What Is an American?" in *Letters from an American Farmer and Sketches of 18th Century America* (New York: New American Library, 1963).

12. Alexis de Tocqueville, "Township and Municipal Decentralization," in *Democracy in America*, trans. Henry Reeve (London: Saunders & Otley, 1840), I, v.

13. Tocqueville, "Associations in Civil Life," in *Democracy in America*, trans. Henry Reeve (London: Saunders & Otley, 1840), II, 2, v.

14. *The Federalist Papers*, No. 9.

Chapter Five

Early Constitutional Issues

IS DIVISION OF POWER PHILOSOPHICALLY UNSOUND?

Why was it that the whole idea of the American government—its separation of powers—rejected, even ridiculed, by most of the serious thinkers of the day, and still is today by many, if not most, intellectuals worldwide? Why did almost every philosopher in the old world believe that the new government could not work? There were four major reasons.

First, as noted, they believed that the "dualism," upon which the whole Constitution was based, was sloppy thinking, not philosophical, and irrational.[1] They said it contradicted the first principle of logic. There must be one first principle, not two. The first principle of government was sovereignty, to concentrate its power to achieve national greatness. The Founders divided power because they were fearful, not heroic about empowering the state to guarantee justice. All American common sense could respond to the charge was that more of the world's people (Christians—and Hindus, too) believed in the idea of multiplicity, even in their Godhead, than in any other single belief. So, it made sense to them too.

As far as logic was concerned, Aristotle actually made "happiness" the first premise of his philosophy of human nature and society. It was Aristotle's and Thomas' critics who called this dualism, because happiness was deemed by the critics as too vague to be a "real" first principle. So, its second principles of spiritual and material happiness were considered as its joint first principles and, thus, labeled "dual." Aristotle and Thomas, however, viewed their philosophy logically based upon the first premise of human beings seeking happiness, from which followed the "dualism" of natural and supernatural or noble happiness.[2]

Second, no government could act rationally if someone was not in charge, the critics argued. As Woodrow Wilson put it, the separation of powers was "manifestly a radical defect on our federal system in that it parcels out power and confuses responsibility."[3] The popular response was that the divided American government did act and its survival today as the oldest continuing constitution in the world proved its reasonableness. This is not a logical proof but 200 years of successful activity is a common sense rebuke to the claim that may or may not be convincing, depending upon the point of view.

Third, the Founders and Locke placed the principle of liberty prior to that of justice. Yet, it is impossible to argue logically that freedom must lead to justice. There must be a plan, Plato and the others argued, in order to guarantee justice. Otherwise, liberty allowed freedom for evil too. History proved this, from corrupt Athens to the Holocaust. That freedom can be abused is true, so all American common sense could reply was that its people think freedom works and millions around the world seem to want to come there to experience it.

Finally, freedom clearly relies upon support from religion, for without some such internal, moral control, there would be anarchy which a strong central mechanism would seek to control.[4] As George Washington expressed it, "religion and morality are indispensable supports" of "free government."[5] But religion was false, myth according to Nietzsche and the others, and that means freedom and the American system are built upon sand. Again, the only answer is the commonsensical one that most Americans and other peoples of the world do have faith in a religion. Why is it not possible they are right and maybe Nietzsche is wrong?

But none of this is proof. Except on dualism, they are not even philosophical responses, much less correct ones. Common sense is not enough. Still, Americans have historically found common sense, whether it seems to work, a satisfactory justification—whether, in fact, it is sufficient for such a conclusion or not.

DID THE BALANCE WORK?

Did the new divided government actually work? Madison anticipated that different views of religion, government, leadership, and especially property would sunder the population and threaten the survival of its government. Yet, he also thought that the new government could manage that conflict through rational discussion covered with good will within a divided and decentralized administration.[6] In fact, in the early United States, territorial development and settlement, tariffs, a national bank, internal improvements, foreign alliances, and so forth divided the population.[7] Some issues were resolved nationally and others not. Around the most profound differences, political parties were developed, with Thomas Jefferson himself leading the way in creating the world's first mass-based national and democratic political organization. The divided government survived its potential logical weaknesses by leaving most of social life, and even government, to private and local institutions, which performed the overwhelming amount of the work. Whatever the rational merits, a prosperity and diversity followed that satisfied those already settled there and attracted many more from abroad, vastly increasing the population and the nation's prospects.

Very early in its history, the national government did begin to grow beyond its enumerated Constitutional functions—primarily building "internal improvements" like canals and roads and creating a national bank—but these were arguably interstate commerce or "post roads" or related to coining money, functions listed in the Constitution. In fact, more than 90 percent of government remained local even through the 19th century as private business grew several times larger even than local and voluntary government as time went on. There were even some retrenchments in the growth of government—Jefferson and Madison wrote the Virginia and Kentucky resolutions to limit national power, Andrew Jackson repealed the national bank charter, Warren Harding and Calvin Coolidge returned to "normalcy" and less government after World War I, Dwight Eisenhower ended wage and price controls and cut government controls after World War II, and Ronald Reagan reduced domestic national government in the 1980s from 17.9 to 16.6 percent of GDP. Yet, the long-term trend was to expand national power and responsibility, for more national government involvement in formerly state, local, and private matters.

Whatever the challenges and changes, the new American government proved itself reasonably successful in resolving the normal conflicts that arose. But problems of equality, as de Tocqueville predicted, challenged the new government and society in unique ways and, in one manifestation, came to threaten its very existence.

IS THE VOTE THE MEASURE?

Both Locke and Madison emphasized that this new national government must be based upon popular consent to be considered legitimate. But what does this mean—that all people must have equal power, that all issues must be decided by town meeting or referenda, that all people must be able to vote, that only native or naturalized citizens may vote, that the vote can be denied to the very young or to criminals, or perhaps even to those without a financial stake in the community? However defined, voting is an important aspect of popular consent. Under the Constitution, voting qualifications were determined mostly by the states and many imposed property qualifications, although the democratic spirit always created pressure to eliminate them. Many voting restrictions on property were removed as early as President Andrew Jackson but a few remain for some elections even today.

How much political equality was required, strangely, was not universally accepted and was debated from the beginning. Is formal voting real power or is real power the ability to influence those who make the decisions? While not disputing the importance of the vote, John Adams raised the issue to Thomas Jefferson in their correspondence late in life, whether aristocracies always rule even in democracies?[8] Adams argued that they do, because leadership in positions of power is based upon virtues and talents. These differences include wealth, birth, genus, virtue, education, strength, beauty, and so forth. These talents are recognized whether there are elections or not, affecting who is leader, wins votes, or influences the laws that are adopted for the nation.

The talented rise to the top. In any assembly of 100, 25 or fewer will have more of these qualities and these will lead. These are "aristocrats" to Adams—those who lead naturally for whatever reason. The great democrat, Jefferson, comes to agree with Adams as long as leadership is not artificially closed by the law.[9] Birth aristocracies are always corrupt and only succeed if they are propped up by government rules. However, some of these natural leaders are corrupt, so virtue is essential among the leaders if the nation is to be successful, whether selected by their neighbors or not. But how can one guarantee this?

The secret to avoiding corruption is to limit everyone's power. Because America did, Adams predicted the U.S. would hold out "many hundreds of years" before corruption and demagoguery would undermine its institutions. He even argued that women could be part of this natural aristocracy and specifically mentioned Lady Hamilton—rising from the streets to preserve a free Europe by socially and intellectually supporting its savior, Horatio Nelson—and several others, claiming there were "millions" of other examples of women with real power even if they did not vote.

FEMALE SUFFRAGE: VOTE OR MIND?

His wife, Abigail Adams did not agree. The question of how women should participate in the new government was one of the earliest issues. Abigail Adams was a strong proponent of female legal equality and the necessity for female education. She was disappointed that the "ladies" were not mentioned in the Constitution,[10] but like most of the rest of the government, most of the action on participation was at the state or local level. The Constitution gave the states the right to set voting qualifications, but at the state level, there was little sympathy for female suffrage. Still, independent-minded women like her persevered in their demands from the outset.

Contemporary, Mary Wollstonecraft, mother of talented and educated Mary Shelly—author of *Frankenstein* and wife of poet Percy—was even more forceful and comprehensive in her claim for female equality. Equality, however, essentially meant equality of the mind to both of these leading women. Wollstonecraft, especially, set reason as the standard and the goal for women, not equality. She conceded women were not equal in strength. She even concluded that if it turned out women were not mentally equal, that would be fine, if they were judged on the basis of their ability to reason and not as a group. She even argued that the philosopher Jean Jacques Rousseau could be right about man being the natural leader but only if he could prove it rationally, which he clearly had not.[11]

By 1848, enough women were desirous of legal equality that a convention could be convened in Seneca Falls, New York. Elizabeth Cady Stanton composed a whole new "Declaration of Sentiments" modeled on the Declaration of Independence to make the case for female equality, even arguing that women must get rid of the advantages for themselves that currently existed in the law and be equal with men even where they were now given special benefits and protections.[12]

By and large, the issue of female political equality over the vote was fought—and to a great extent won—at the state level during the 19th century, especially in the West. Women won the vote in 1869 in Wyoming, 1893 in Colorado and 1896 in Utah and Idaho. There was limited success in the East until the 20th century when the 19th Amendment finally was passed nationally and uniformly forbade denial of the right to vote on the basis of sex.

The remedy of Wollstonecraft's major concern, equality of the mind in female higher education, started earlier with the opening of Mount Holyoke College in 1837 and, especially of Elmira Female College in 1853, which was the first to provide all of the male-equivalent courses she demanded. Yet, male and female numbers in higher education did not reach equality until the 1980s. By the end of that century, however, there were more women than men enrolled in institutions of higher learning. So, equality in voting and higher education were achieved under the rules of the existing Constitution, even if it took a long time. But this did not necessarily lead to equality in other areas of life, about which we will have more to say later.

SLAVERY: COMPROMISE OR ABOMINATION?

The one issue the new national government could not ignore for very long was slavery—recognized as a major fault line right from the beginning by de Tocqueville, among others. From its earliest days, he was pessimistic that it could be dealt with peacefully under the Constitution, even though he recognized slavery as both against Christianity and economically inefficient and growing more so. "By the choice of the master or the will of the slave, it will cease and in either case great calamities may be expected to ensue."[13]

Only a former slave could probably set the issue more dramatically, as did the great orator of emancipation, Frederick Douglass. In 1845, the newspaper publisher and later public commissioner observed that a slave found it difficult to celebrate the American nation, even on the 4th of July, because the country did not live up to its founding ideals. He was especially critical of Christian ministers who knew better and did not speak up for the principles of their religion that should have declared slavery immoral. Many even distorted those teachings. But he was forceful that Christianity was clear, that all peoples were created equal by God. So how could one people be treated by another as property? In fact, he argued, even the most adamant inadvertently admitted that slaves were human. Why else would they pass laws making certain actions criminal? A piece of property or animal cannot commit a crime. The recently passed Fugitive Slave Law nationalized slavery for the first time, he concluded, proving that matters were getting worse and required action even to keep things from degenerating further for the slave population.[14]

Soon after his 4th of July speech, things did get worse. The Missouri Compromise had admitted Missouri as a slave state but balanced that with the admission of Maine as a free state, while prohibiting any additional slave states north of 36°30'. In 1854, with no hope of admitting Kansas territory in the face of a Southern opposition that feared this would have given the North a permanent majority in the Senate, Steven Douglas introduced a compromise to split it into two states—Kansas and Nebraska—and to decide their status as free or slave by popular vote. In doing this, the Missouri compromise principle of forbidding slavery in the North forever was undermined and anti-slavery forces were determined to overturn it.

In fact, Senator Douglas expected that slavery would be voted down in both states and did not think the Missouri principle was that important. His Senate opponent Abraham Lincoln did but—although he apparently won a small plurality of the popular vote—lost the election between them in the state legislature. Both sides organized to prevail in the Kansas and Nebraska state referenda, which soon degenerated into open war throughout the vast territory.

A national conflict could be avoided no longer, as all balancing broke down. The nation split in two socially—religious, fraternal, charitable, and political organizations broke into Northern and Southern branches, some of which persist to the present. Debates in Congress became contentious and even led to fighting on the floor. Finally, all comity broke down between the regions. The issue was only resolved by civil war, in 1861, following Lincoln's election and the Southern firing on Ft. Sumter.

Could it have been avoided through traditional compromise under the Constitution? The South was still agricultural and the loss of equality in the Senate guaranteed a decline in its power. In order to recognize this impasse, could the national government have purchased the slaves and set them free, for example? Would that have been enough to right the balance? In any event, passions were high and this was not seriously considered.

Abraham Lincoln viewed the resulting four-year war—whose casualties were not exceeded until World War I—for both North and South as "the woe due to those by whom the offense came." During the war, Lincoln took drastic steps to win, including holding 13,535 prisoners without habeas corpus protection—in defiance of the Supreme Court—including 31 Maryland state legislators. The Civil War was not unique in this limitation of habeas rights as Woodrow Wilson's Sabotage and Sedition Act did so too for World War I, for as little as only holding disloyal opinions. In World War II, Franklin Delano Roosevelt detained 110,000 Japanese, of whom 70 percent were citizens—albeit mostly children of non-citizens—and in the recent war against terrorism, George W. Bush held 830 suspected terrorists without allowing habeas corpus protection. Right or wrong, Constitutional or not, rights often take a backseat to questions of security and order in wartime.[15] Finally, the war ended with the North victorious.

The Civil War was fought on the homeland, between its citizens and so had great effect upon America's future. With victory, the North and industry became dominant politically and the South was placed under military control by a Washington-based occupation called Reconstruction. The old state and national dualism was seriously eroded, in fact with the growth of national power during the war and legally afterwards. Slavery was forbidden by the 13th Amendment and, more importantly, the 14th Amendment clearly limited state legal power. The latter, for the first time—other than the procedural "rights of Englishmen" in the Constitution itself—provided for the possibility of uniform individual legal rights across the nation, reversing the general federalist theme.

With the tied 1876 presidential election, the South was able to use its electoral votes to allow the Republicans to win the election in exchange for the removal of occupying troops and the end of Reconstruction. Opening elections to whites in the South resulted in laws against the newly liberated for-mer slaves, and a following Supreme Court decision (*Plessy v. Ferguson*) le-gitimized "separate but equal" public facilities for the two races, making the 14th Amendment unenforceable. The potential for the 14th to limit state power was not exercised until the 20th century to any major degree, which will be considered further below. But questions about the legitimacy of the old federalist regime were raised immediately.

UNIVERSAL EVIL OR CHRISTIAN/WESTERN INVENTION?

What was the role of the Western tradition, the Constitution, and American values generally in supporting the now generally recognized evil of slavery? Of course, until England abolished slavery in 1833, slavery was near univer-sal and not confined to any single race. Even Aristotle justified it. A whole people, the European Slavs, were branded by it. The Ottomans relied almost exclusively upon Christian slaves to populate its administrative class. Euro-peans did manage the African slave trade and operated its slave system, but Western slavery of blacks would not have been possible without Africans first capturing their fellow inhabitants and making the immobilized slaves avail-able for international trade. Europeans did not enter into central Africa until the 19th century and so could not physically do so by themselves.

Early Christianity did not forbid slavery although it taught that slaves should be treated as brothers and sisters. Medieval Christianity generally avoided slavery, and although it substituted serfdom, this was recognized as an advance, even by Marx. Critically, the Western nation England and several other Christian countries in South America were the first to end it. The U.S. did not follow until three decades later, after paying a terrible cost, as Lincoln stressed. But even that was earlier than in most non-Western nations. The strongest case that Western values actually assisted in moving toward the abo-lition of slavery was made by the former slave, Frederick Douglass. He specifically used Christian norms to appeal to those, even ministers, he said were not following its precepts. Critically, he relied almost exclusively upon the Declaration's principles and Christian doctrine to make his case. Later Martin Luther King would do the same against segregation.

Outside of the West, slavery lasted into the 20th century, particularly in the Muslim world. It continues to this day outside the West, as does greater re-pression generally, as is documented by the studies of the subject throughout the world by the generally respected Freedom House annual survey. Slavery still exists in Africa, in Sudan and Mauritania, and related systems like caste survive in Asia, in India, and even to a degree in Japan.

Yet, it cannot be denied that the West tolerated slavery for a very long time. Even afterwards, white majorities in the Southern U.S. adopted ruses to continue many of its restrictions. "Negro Codes" were adopted that segregated the races and did not provide the equality before the law that the Constitution promised.

WESTERN FEMALE OPPRESSION?

Women had no direct, individual political power, except for monarchs, in the West before modern times. Women were universally viewed in the context of the family and raising children. The hand that rocked the cradle ruled the world but not politics, as even monarchs like Queen Victoria were, in theory at least, obedient to their husbands in the recesses of the family. Indeed, the universal American and Western practice until recently was of the individual acting within community, including the family community, not as an isolated individual with separate rights at all. Individualism outside the confines of community was a later innovation, as we shall soon see.

Viewing women only within the family was not unique to the West. Indeed, the status of women had always been higher there than under any other major world tradition. In Islam, a man could have more than one wife, and women often could not go out of the house without being fully covered and accompanied by a male relative. While there were some powerful wives in the Ottoman harem, it was indirectly through husband or son. Both Islam and Hinduism had parents select spouses for children—which was the exception rather than the rule in the West—and Hinduism did not end female child marriage or even suttee until forced to by a Western power in the 19th century. Many native peoples sacrificed virgins and children. Even orthodox Judaism required men and women to worship separately. Few non-Western nations even allowed female monarchs. Christianity taught moral equality of the sexes and gave women access to the highest ranks of their saints, especially Mary, who was only just below God Himself. There were many, many female saints, even a military one, Joan of Arc!

On the other hand, it is clear that Christendom did not teach rights generally for women but stressed obligations for both men and women. Even Locke gave more emphasis to obligations than rights, especially in the family, where there were obligations for both sexes. While the Christian injunction to woman was to follow her husband, the husband was to follow Jesus, certainly the more difficult task since he was crucified. In the West, the family was considered the first and most essential social institution, one that needed to be protected by law. "Family voting" as part of an unbreakable unit was considered one of those protections—together with great difficulty for the man to obtain divorce or to leave his wife without abandoning a large share of his estate, or even female immunity from aspects of the criminal law for crimes committed with the knowledge of the husband. Of course, as John Adams noted, there was indirect female power, too. But direct participation proved elusive.

Even the indomitable Elizabeth Cady Stanton could only win 100 of 300 people at her convention of two-thirds women to support her "Declaration of Sentiments"! And some of those who had supported it later removed their signatures. It is important to recall that her Declaration proposed to remove legal advantages from women, including barriers to male divorce and immunity from some crimes—which immunity she said made women morally "irresponsible." But many women did not agree with her about these matters at the time and for long afterwards.

By the early 20th century, women changed their mind and supported much of the Stanton program and achieved victory when the Constitution was amended in 1920 to allow women to vote. Yet, Mary Wollstonecraft and Abigail Adams thought higher education was more important than voting. The fact that there are more women than men in higher education today would undoubtedly please them more. Still, some of the older reservations linger. A woman, Phyllis Schlafly, led a successful effort to defeat a full female equal rights amendment to the Constitution in the late-20th century, arguing that it would make women subject to a military draft and even to common lavatory facilities. As recently as September 29, 2001, Kansas State Senator Kay O'Connor said, while she would not repeal it today, the passage of the 19th Amendment took away legal protections from women—such as fault-limited divorce, guaranteed custody of children after divorce, and alimony and full shares of fortunes in separations—and so was a sign people did not value family solidarity highly enough.

THE NEW INDIVIDUALISM: RIGHTS OVER RESPONSIBILITY?

Much of the justification for female legal equality was drawn from a new idea of individualism that placed the individual over the family, community, and government as the highest social entity, over all other institutional social and legal norms. This new doctrine of liberated individualism was best expressed at the time by the American philosophers Ralph Waldo Emerson and Henry Thoreau. Emerson specifically rejected virtue in its Aristotelian communal sense, what he derisively called "the popular estimate." To be an individual, one must be a nonconformist, he argued, not follow the government, community, family, tradition, religion, or the crowd.

In case anyone missed the point of individual over community, he asked: "Is not a man better than a town?" Even mother and father were shunned for individual emancipation. Indeed, "no law is sacred to me but that of my nature." Consistency itself is labeled "the hobgoblin of little minds." Sympathy is base, and sensitivity should be substituted for with "truth and health in rough electric shocks." In the end, "nothing is at last sacred but the integrity of your own mind." Just "obey your heart" becomes his only moral rule.[16]

Emerson and Thoreau changed how many Americans thought about rights—as things the law guaranteed to individuals, no matter what the competing family, community, or governmental claims. This contrasted sharply with the older, dualist, "communal individualism" earlier identified by de Tocqueville. This older, social individualism of community, town, family, and voluntary association began to wane following the disruption of local ties after the centralization and industrialism spurred by the Civil War, but it was not really overridden until the early 20th century.

In many ways, this debate between the older and newer individualism became the central issue for the nation's future, continuing as a live issue to this very day. Who is more correct—is it Emerson, or is it de Tocqueville or Wollstonecraft or Douglass, or is it someone else?

NOTES

1. Leo Strauss, "Marsilius of Padua," in Leo Strauss and Joseph Cropsey, eds., *History of Philosophy* (Chicago: Rand McNally, 1963), 227–46.

2. Aristotle, *Nichomachean Ethics*, trans. Davis Ross (London: Oxford University Press, 1925), 1:10.

3. Woodrow Wilson, *Congressional Government* (New York: Meridian Books, 1956). Also see Donald Devine, "American Culture and Public Administration," *Policy Studies Journal* (December 1982), 255–60.

4. F. A. Hayek, *The Fatal Conceit* (Chicago: University of Chicago Press, 1988), chap. 9.

5. George Washington, Farewell Address.

6. *The Federalist Papers*, No. 10.

7. William H. Young, *Ogg and Ray's Introduction to American Government* (New York: Meredith, 1962); Paul Johnson, *A History of the American People* (New York: Harper-Collins, 1997); Steven F. Hayward, *The Age of Reagan* (Roseville, Calif.: Prima, 2001); and Michael Barone, *Our Country* (New York: The Free Press, 1990) are used extensively as historical references.

8. John and Abigail Adams, *The Book of Abigail and John* (Cambridge; Harvard University Press, 1975), 15 November 1813. David McCullough, *John Adams*, (New York: Simon & Schuster, 2001), 600–608.

9. Thomas Jefferson, *Letters 1787–1883*, letter dated 28 October 1813.

10. Abgail Adams, *The Book of Abigail and John*, letter dated 31 March 1776.

11. Mary Wollstonecraft, *A Vindication of the Rights of Women* (London: J. P. Johnson, 1792).

12. Elizabeth Cady Stanton, *Declaration of Sentiments* (New York: R. J. Johnson, 1870).

13. Tocqueville, "Present and Future of the Negro," in *Democracy in America*, trans. Henry Reeve (London: Saunders & Otley, 1840), I: xviii, 372–75.

14. Frederick Douglass, "What to a Slave Is the Fourth of July?" speech delivered at the Corinthian Hall in Rochester, New York, 4 July 1852. Actually most of the Founders were not favorable to slavery. Benjamin Franklin and Benjamin Rush founded America's first anti-slavery society in 1774. Supreme Court Justice John Jay was president of a similar society in New York. Prominent Founders who were active in such societies included Charles Carroll, Richard Stockton, James Madison, Richard Bassett, William Few, James Monroe, Bushrod Washington, John Marshall, Zephaniah Swift, and many more. Pennsylvania and Massachusetts abolished slavery in 1780; Connecticut and Rhode Island in 1784; New Hampshire in 1792; Vermont in 1793; New York in 1799; and New Jersey in 1804. Moreover, many Founders who had owned slaves later released them: George Washington, George Wythe, Ceasar Rodney, William Livingston and John Dickinson. "America's Founders Are Still Heroes," *Omaha World-Herald*, 23 February 2002.

15. Abraham Lincoln, Second Inaugural Address; Johnson, *A History of the American People*, 4–88, 307–25, 429–95, and 500–507; and Pew Research Center, *Terror Coverage Boosts News Media: But Military Censorship Boosted* (Washington, D.C.: 2001).

16. Ralph Waldo Emerson, "Self-Reliance," in *Essays* (Boston: Munne, 1841).

Chapter Six

Community, Government, and Individual Responsibility

THE CHALLENGE TO THE OLD REPUBLIC

With the problem of civil rights for former slaves in the background, the Civil War sacrifices and increased national government presence still fresh in mind, industrialization and urbanization becoming the new way of life, and a spirit of individualism set free from community as a new competing vision—the old local, divided, federalist, dualist regime was put in question. Both the war and the 14th Amendment placed the sovereignty of the states as a debatable proposition. Centralization, industrialization, and urbanization turned loyalties from localities and voluntary associations to individuals, including corporate "persons," and a more active national government, which gave as its central justification that it would protect both types of individuals.

While none of these issues were resolved at the time, the once-unquestioned Constitution had become the subject of debate. While the union had prevailed militarily and governmentally, it had also failed—either in whether it should have allowed slavery in the first place or whether it simply could not peacefully resolve the most important question put before it. The old issue of the relationship between the individual, community, and the state—of the type of government that was best—was raised anew not a century after the original Constitution had been considered the final word on the subject of American government.

What alternatives might there be? We will consider seven major views of the relationship of the individual to the community and government, ones that have provided the basis for the permanent debate over what is the best form of government.

SEVEN GOVERNMENTAL ALTERNATIVES

Government Is Power

In the story of Gyges, Socrates' cynical debating partner Glaucon presented the argument that individuals always act solely in their own personal interest, with no obligation to community or state except what is useful for selfish reasons.[1] The proof was that anyone who had Gyges' power to become invisible by rubbing his enchanted ring would act as selfishly as he did, doing whatever he wished with no one the wiser. With that magic ring's power, Gyges killed the king and became ruler of all. Power is what counts, and that is what community and government are all about. Rulers have power and use it to their personal advantage, just as any other human would. While average citizens do not have great power, they act as sharply as they can for their advantage, as much as they can without getting caught. Justice is simply the mean between the "best of all, which is to do injustice and not be punished, and the worst of all, which is to suffer injustice without the power of retaliation." Government and its justice are not good, as Socrates claimed, but are tolerated as the "lesser evil." People act "justly" only if forced to do so, by government. There is not community obligation, but fear, avoidance, and self-interest are the motivators in government, for both the ruler and the ruled. It is raw power against raw power.

Government Is Community

The Jewish prophet and judge Samuel, on the contrary, argued that true justice—that is, treating all fairly, not selfishly in one's own interest—is demanded from all by God, who will not be mocked. Individuals must follow God's commands freely and absolutely and reject self-interest or suffer the consequences. Humanity can overcome evil and achieve the good only if it freely follows God's will. Loyalty must be to God over every other thing, including the government. Samuel even argued against establishing government in the community of Israel at all because individuals should be responsible only and directly to God. Law should be enforced by Him and His people without formal officials or constitutions. When the people demanded a king for Israel from Samuel, God told him the people had rejected God by making that request.[2]

If the people followed God's law, the community did not require a state, as Israel had not experienced until then. The judges simply made decisions based upon God's law, and God or the community carried out the judgment. There were no formal government officials, police, or standing army. God told Samuel to warn the people about the dangers and evils of the state but said to agree to a king if they insisted. Once they had conceded the power to the government, however, the leaders would lord it over the community, and the people would bear the costs. It would have been better to continue having God as ruler over a free community than suffer the abuses that inevitably will occur under an institutionalized government. But they asked for it and will obey and pay the consequences.

Government Is Guile

The man many call the first true political scientist, Niccolo Machiavelli, confirmed Samuel's worst fears by teaching in a most convincing and comprehensive way that neither God nor the free community are important in the state. People are selfish, as Glaucon proved, but they must be controlled or there will be no peace. Yet, rulers cannot rely upon raw power because groups and families are too powerful. So, rulers must manipulate people to follow the law. The wise ruler knows how to appear compassionate but to act with guile to keep order and maintain his own power.[3] The model for the ruler is the lion and the fox, to be powerful and sly. Contrary to Samuel, government is the essential institution to provide order. Government consists of its leaders, however, not its community, no matter what the formal constitution. Even in a democracy, political leaders have the power to manipulate the masses and can get around elections by bribing the people with popular programs. Elections actually only choose between two sets of leaders, not set policy. The point is for leaders to use power wisely to stay on top, heedless of all other considerations. The political leader's self-interest does have a beneficial community effect in that it is in his interest to keep order. The people can never rule for they cannot be ruthless and far-seeing enough. But they do demand law and order. Only princes, either hereditary or elected, have the skill and ambition to rise to the top and the iron will to manipulate events enough to keep enemies at bay and to keep the people satisfied enough to keep them in power.

Government Is the General Will

The great French philosopher, Jean J. Rousseau, held that Samuel was correct that only the community could give moral authority to a government. Power, even if crafty, cannot legitimize. But no modern, rational person could accept God as a basis for legitimacy either. Only a state of nature, where man lives uncorrupted by civilization, exists prior to government, so only this community had the ability to transfer its moral authority to another institution such as the state. On the other hand, Machiavelli was also partially correct. In modern times, the state and political leadership are necessary if any communal action is to be effective. To be legitimate today, then, leaders must operate under a "social contract" from the community. The community's "general will" sets the proper goals for society, not what the leader selfishly desires. While leaders must interpret that will, they do so under the democratic scrutiny of the people in a manner that unites people and leaders.

Since authority comes from the people, the state must be single-minded in following this general will. All laws and actions must be for the common good and implemented directly in accord with that common will. Since there was no God to establish a moral system, and there must be proper values for the people to follow or there will be social chaos, a successful government must devise, based upon the general will, a simple, rational, neutral state religion that defines the values under which the state and its citizens must act and govern themselves. The government must not be undermined by compromises with special interests. It must not be divided by different powers or institutions or interests or cults, especially any that explicitly divide religion from the state, but must always follow the values of the uniform common will. As the violent history of Christian Europe has proved, divided loyalty between state and religion leads to great disorder.[4]

Government Is Limited and Consensual.

The Declaration of Independence presented the rationale for the old American form of government and society. It, following Rousseau, appealed to values beyond the state or its rulers, to the people and even to the community of mankind. But it went further, indeed outside the world altogether, also following Samuel, to "the supreme judge of the world" for its legitimacy. God was not dead for America's Founders. While not all signers were orthodox Christians, most were and all agreed that individual rights came from and were justified only by the fact of a Creator. He endowed individuals with "unalienable rights," and governments were to be evaluated based upon how well they secured those rights. Only by placing those rights in a place human power could not reach could they remain secure from encroachment, especially from government. It was the fact that these Creator's rights were abused that was used to justify breaking from the established government of England—confirming Rousseau's fear regarding the dangerousness of Christian imagery for the stability of the state.

Contra Machiavelli, rulers did not have unlimited rights, but governments must be based upon limited constitutions that reflect the "consent of the governed" and protect life, liberty, and the pursuit of private happiness. As the Federalist noted, people have angelic and fallen natures. To protect from abuse, government is required. To allow people to exercise their freedom to act beneficially, government must be limited. Contra Rousseau, factions must be tolerated, including multiple religious sects, and granted substantial freedom from the state, whose job is to control their violent expressions only under rules that apply equally to all. Mostly, order must be maintained by these private institutions and individuals. If government exceeded its rightful powers, the people could overthrow it. Independence, however, was not an abstract matter of what a general will desired or universal rights demanded, but it was only justified by specific enumerated insults against "one [concrete] people" by rulers taking specific abusive acts that were sufficient to justify revolution. Governments could not be changed for light or transient causes: Only "a long train of abuses and usurpations" could justify overthrowing the community's government. As long as the government generally respected the Creator-given rights, the citizen was obliged to obey.

Government Is Unnatural and Should Be Resisted by Individuals

Emerson and Thoreau's new individualism rejected this idea that the individual had an obligation to obey the government. No law is sacred to me, proclaimed Emerson; individuals were only required to follow their own hearts. Government "can have no pure right over my person and property but what I concede it," proclaimed Thoreau. No force, no God, no community, no neutral judge, no majority, no outside standard, no separation of powers could justify state action against the individual's will. Not even substantial abuses were required to refuse obedience to the state. Thoreau objected to a few cent tax and refused to pay it on principle. Any action the state takes without the consent of every individual is unjust and need not be obeyed. "That government is best that governs not at all," was Thoreau's motto for government and for all communities.[5]

Government Is Universal

The United Nations' Universal Declaration of Human Rights did not make individual rights dependent upon a Creator, nor upon the rights, values, or institutions specific to one community, nation, or people, nor upon power, nor even on individualism. It declared a universal "inherent dignity" that resides in each person because he or she was a member of the "human family."[6] Universal rights stand upon their own universal moral authority. They do not need outside support, neither from religion nor any particular community morality nor tradition. The rights specified in the U.N. Declaration are more extensive than those of the U.S. Declaration's and require more positive government action than Thoreau or the U.S. Founders would support. Rousseau might urge that the General Assembly of all the United Nations, where each nation has one vote no matter the size or strength of the nation, be given the power if these more extensive rights are to be secured as the general will of the peoples of the world. But Machiavelli might note that the U.N. can only enforce them with the unanimous support of the five powerful permanent members of its Security Council.

RESPONSIBILITY TO COMMUNITY AND GOVERNMENT: IS THERE ANY?

So, what is the relationship between the individual, community, and government? Glaucon, Machiavelli, Emerson, and Thoreau positively reject the idea that individuals have any moral responsibility to anyone or any institution except for themselves, beyond the degree they themselves consider right and prudent. Government is, at best, a necessary evil that must be avoided or manipulated. It is obeyed only because it has the power to compel lawfulness. The United Nations promulgates rights, but it too is silent about moral responsibility. To Samuel, moral responsibility is all that is required and one does not even need a state. Rousseau requires responsibility, but it is communal and secular, not individual. The Declaration of Independence is unique in using both the language of pledging individual honor to sacred, enduring principles and securing a specific government for a given people. This dual sense of responsibility reaches back to Aristotle, who argued that "man is born to citizenship" in family, community, and state and that individual responsibility to all is natural to the species. Individual happiness is the highest goal, but virtue, which leads to happiness, must be developed in the community. The good and meaningful life consists in pursuing duty to one's neighbors and family within the society of the city community.[7]

Aristotle recognized in his *Ethics* that people differ over the meaning of happiness—pleasure, honor, money, and contemplation were all mentioned as examples. But these were not desired for their own sake since nothing can be the chief good if it is secondary to something else. People wanted the happiness resulting from these things, not the things for their own sakes. So, happiness itself was the highest good. It only reached its perfection when "life [was] desirable and lacking in nothing." To reach this perfection, it was not enough to contemplate the Ideal of virtue, as with Plato, for sloth was not virtuous. Action was required. But this difference with Plato was not critical since active virtue was obviously a sub-category of virtue generally, which both agreed constituted the only "permanent" happiness. Politics was the highest calling because it sought the highest virtue, the happiness of all citizens.

Happiness must be satisfying not only in community but also "when isolated." To be noble, a person seeks pleasure only in doing what is held as virtuous by the community even when outside of its laws. Even when this individual is in pain, "nobility shines through" because noble or heroic virtue is accomplished with "greatness of soul." Aristotle's principle of happiness thus requires both a body and a soul for, even if the body is not happy in suffering, the soul can be still said to be happy after a life of virtue by bearing difficulties nobly, heroically, even in death. Indeed, do we not recognize nobility of soul most when it overcomes pain and suffering, as the hero does on the battlefield for his neighbors or in rescuing another from harm? A deeper, nobler happiness than simple pleasure shines through in these lives.

Of course, many moderns reject the very idea of soul or virtue and any duty that might follow from them. Gyges and the rest dismiss the idea of happiness in pain as impossible to accept and so they can continue to reject the necessity for virtue, or even only for individual responsibility, as foolish. Even Thomas Aquinas considered Aristotle's formulation impossible for a self-interested human to bear and said an afterlife would be necessary to give final and real happiness to those who died in heroic pain. Locke considered this the major attraction of Christianity to the masses: it provided substance to Aristotle's abstract explanation, that there was a real reward in Heaven for the virtuous, especially for those who died in pain, as did its founder.[8]

Whatever the qualifications, it is clear that the Declaration of Independence followed Aristotle in making the pursuit of happiness the goal of human life. For Aristotle, Thomas, Locke, and the Declaration, happiness is the first and ruling principle. While their opponents considered the happiness of the soul as the highest principle a "platitude"—in Aristotle's own term for how his opponents would characterized him[9]—and "dualistic," the American Founders clearly sided with Aristotle that happiness required virtue, duty to neighbor, community and government, and even the willingness to sacrifice lives and fortunes in its pursuit.

WHAT KIND OF RESPONSIBILITY IS REQUIRED, IF ANY?

The ideal of the noble soul has inspired much of Western teaching and literature. Socrates gave his life rather than offend virtue. Many of the prophets were killed. Jesus died for the sins of mankind on the cross. The martyrs sacrificed their lives. Heroic military and political leaders became the ideal: Ulysses, Gideon, Arthur, Cincinnatus, Charlemagne, El Cid, Richard the Lionhearted, St. Joan, and the like heroically devoted their energies to the community. At least until recently, these and others representing the heroic virtues were taught to children to be emulated in their own lives. Western poetry also lauded the romantic alternative of the lover of the soil and beauty, the conventional yeoman farmer, the ordinary democratic citizen, and the frugal Yankee, who eschewed heroism and stressed the practical—epitomized by Benjamin Franklin's Poor Richard. But it should be noted that the supposedly practical Franklin did step to the plate for the Revolution and put his life on the line with the others.[10]

To the founding generation, George Washington exemplified all of these ideals as even Thomas Jefferson, who often was a political rival, willingly admitted. In his teens, Washington was in demand as a surveyor of the frontier, by twenty he was adjutant of one of four Virginia military districts, by 22 was commander of the Virginia Regiment, led the Continental Army during the Revolution, presided over the Constitutional Convention, and was unanimously elected first president of his new country. He set his slaves free upon his death. Washington was pictured as the heroic man of the soil, serving his God, his community, and his government with courage, prudence, and virtue. In fact, his countrymen considered him "first in war, first in peace and first in the hearts of his countrymen," as one contemporary put it.[11] More recently, Martin Luther King, Jr., has been made an heroic example, in his case publicly demonstrating courage in the face of injustice and hatred and going to jail for his convictions.[12] His use of a boycott—a non-coercive method—also showed his practical wisdom in choosing a legal means to protest, achieving a great measure of public sympathy as a consequence, especially at the onset of his struggle.

Many believe this early American ideal of the virtuous, morally responsible soul, who can moderate passions through self-control and religion in the service of the community, as pictured by de Tocqueville and lived by Washington, is an anachronism. Who today does not simply follow whatever his or her heart says is right, in the steps of the more modern philosophers Nietzsche, Emerson, Thoreau, and the rest? Who can say authoritatively that there is a duty to the government or the community? Is not Glaucon/Gyges right that all are out for themselves, and we might as well be so too? How can Aristotle with his ephemeral idea of the soul justify an obligation to suffer to be happy? How can even traditional religion rouse that degree of commitment? Christianity's addition of the "weight" of Jesus' resurrection, and that proof that the soul will be rewarded, may have impressed Locke as sufficient to make the calculation to act morally rational, but what thoroughly modern individual thinks this is sufficient to risk his life? Do not more follow Nietzsche and consider nobility of the soul as simple myth?

What happens in the real world even to those who might accept the ideal in theory when these ideals clash with real danger, as the threat to American young men of serving in the war in Vietnam and the consequent wide avoidance of the military draft in the 1960s generation? Does this not prove Gyges was right that self-interest will prevail? Has 9/11 really changed anything— if a draft proved necessary, would students today act differently? If not, is modern individualism compatible with responsibility? What is there today that justifies duty to family, friends, neighbors, community, or government?

Heroic virtue has had a difficult time in the modern era. At best, "role models" have taken the place of heroes after "improved modes of character assassination, media hype artists and scholars" have performed their leveling function to destroy the idea of heroism, as writer Jenny Bader has observed.[13] Even if only manners are substituted for virtue as necessary for order,[14] it is not clear manners can survive without self-control either, and manners are a long way from Aristotle's noble soul, much less Ulysses' or Washington's self-sacrificing heroism. The question today is whether heroism, morality, good citizenship, duty, family, community, or even decent manners can be justified in any way for the modern world.

NOTES

1. Plato, Gyges, *The Republic*.
2. Book of Samuel, 1: 8.
3. Niccolo Machavelli, *The Prince*, (London: J. M. Dent & Sons, 1908), chaps. X, XIV-XX, XXV.
4. Jean-Jacques Rousseau, "The Social Contract," in *The Social Contract and Discourses and Other Essays*, trans. G. D. H. Cole (New York: Everyman's Library, 1950), chap. 8.
5. Henry David Thoreau, *Resistance to Civil Government* (New Haven, Conn.: Rollins, 1928).
6. United Nations, Universal Declaration of Human Rights.(Lake Success, N.Y.: United Nations, 1949).
7. Aristotle, *Nichomachean Ethics*, trans. Davis Ross (London: Oxford University Press, 1925), I: 1–10.
8. John Locke, *The Reasonableness of Christianity* (Chicago: Regnery Gateway, 1965), 184 and 245.
9. Aristotle, *Nichomachean Ethics*, I: 7.
10. E.g., Alfred Lord Tennyson, "Ulyssus," in *English Idols and Other Poems* (London: King, 1842); Franklin, *The Way to Wealth*; Wendell Berry, "The Man Born to Farming," in *Farming: A Handbook* (New York: Harcourt, Brace Javanovich, 1970).

11. Thomas Jefferson, "The Character of George Washington," in *Letters*, 357–58; Paul Johnson, *A History of the American People* (New York: Harper-Collins, 1997), 121–94.

12. Martin Luther King, *Letter from a Birmingham Jail* (Atlanta: Estate of Martin Luther King, Jr., 1963).

13. Jenny Lynn Bader, "Larger Than Life," in Eric Liu, ed., *Next: Young American Writers on the New Generation* (New York: Norton, 1994).

14. Judith Martin, "The Oldest Virtue," in Glendon and Blankenhorn, ed., *Seedbeds of Virtue* (New York: Madison, 1995).

Chapter Seven

The Market, Freedom, and Spontaneous Order

WHY NOT FREEDOM?

If people will not accept responsibility, why not let everyone be free to do whatever they want with no community or governmental duties at all? In fact, Locke, Rousseau, and many other philosophers assumed that, at the beginning, all people were free. Yet, while born free, everywhere since then there was government and rules restricting freedom. While the Israel of the judges lasted a long time, even Samuel ultimately could not preserve the community from state control. Rousseau, who promoted the moral superiority of the unorganized, natural community, was forced to concede the state was necessary in modern times. The only way to return to freedom, Marx argued, was to eliminate the need for government, which was only required to protect private property, particularly that of the ruling class. When private property was eliminated, individuals could be free, but until then they were everywhere in chains.

As Locke saw it, God granted freedom to every individual in a "state of nature," where he was given the freedom to dispose of life and property "as he wishes." But even then, there was a catch. For each man was expected to use that freedom responsibly for God's moral ends, according to His laws, and He would punish him in the next world if he did not. Man's reason added that individual moral restraint was essential if there was to be any room for freedom in society. Although each individual was free, no one had the moral right to improperly impose on another's liberty or no one could enjoy any freedom. Reason and duty also required one to support one's family and even neighbors in need, for who else could? Even free contracts and agreements had to be considered morally binding or, if broken, subject to damages owed to the injured party, or why would anyone trade?

The problem was that the next life was a long way off and reason did not necessarily lead to following God's law. So, moral law could not be enforced. The difficulty of the heroic life, as Locke noted, was that "it is very unsafe, very insecure." So "the great and chief end" of "men uniting into commonwealths and putting themselves under government, is the preservation of their property."[1] Property was the reason for government, as with Marx, but Locke argued that everyone wanted peace, not just the wealthy. All men freely give up their natural liberty and join a government to gain safety and order in their social and economic life. Indeed, government can only be considered legitimate if all individuals freely give their consent to transfer this power to the state. That government also had obligations, to be bound by the rules that were consented to when it was created. Government may take or regulate one's property only within certain laws made known to all beforehand. Otherwise, no one would join the government freely to make his situation worse than it was in nature. The government must create known, fair rules that respect private freedom, contracts, property, and the fruits of one's labor so that all have greater happiness and security. The obligations are so important that, if the government breaks them in serious matters, all bets are off.

The American Founders, being very influenced by Locke, likewise started with the idea of natural and Creator-granted rights to life, liberty, and property that required popular consent from a people if a government could be considered legitimate. Indeed, to them, to protect freedom and the unequal differences in property that directly followed from liberty was "the first object of government."[2] One of the major failures of the earlier government was the insecurity of property and contract under its rules. While most of property law was left to the states, which contrary to the Founders' fears also tended to be guided by the same Lockean principles, the Fifth Amendment specifically made the protection of property one of the major rights under the new Constitution.

The result of this Lockean synthesis of freedom and natural law was not pure freedom but only limited liberty within consented-to rules enforced by government. Neither Locke nor the Founders planned a free market economy but supported a political constitution based upon freedom; the protection of private property and contract; known, fair, and moral rules; and what they considered were natural political rights. The Founders formed a governmental rather than an economic system. Certain economic consequences followed from these presumptions but they were the result, not the plan. A legal system based upon these principles simply provided a framework within which a particular form of economy naturally developed, one based upon the relatively free exchange of goods and services.

A PRACTICAL ECONOMIC SYSTEM BASED
UPON FREEDOM AND PROPERTY?

Economics looks at the exchange of goods and services as a practical matter of producing wealth rather than as the consequence of following proper political principles. Adam Smith, the Scottish professor who wrote his masterpiece *The Wealth of Nations* in the same year as the American Revolution, started not with natural rights to freedom and property but with actual "natural sentiments" he found deep within human nature (with God there somewhere). These sentiments led people to work for their own and family interests, save to support them, seek approval from neighbors, and even assist their needy neighbors as the decent thing all humans do. On the basis of his analysis, he concluded that governments would simply be prudent to take these sentiments into account in their operations if they desired to be wealthy and prosperous. The individual naturally follows his self-interest, but in this he is "led by an invisible hand to promote an end which was no part of his intention," frequently promoting "society more effectively than when he really intends to promote it." This invisible market was able to perform incredibly complex and enriching tasks more efficiently than any government plan.

As teacher Leonard E. Read explained, even the making of the simple pencil is a task that no one person has the knowledge to perform. It takes many people in a market. No one person knows how to grow and harvest the trees most efficiently in Oregon; manufacture the saws and vehicles required in their fabrication; grow and produce the hemp to haul it; run the logging camps; create, forge, and manage the railways to ship them to California; apply the skills to the millwork within the thickness of less than a quarter inch; run the waxworks and paint kilns; provide the power and oil; mine the graphite in Ceylon; ship and mix it with the clay from Mississippi; press and lacquer (what is that formula?) it together; clasp it with brass from copper and zinc from mines around the world; top it with rubber from the East Indies; and distribute and sell it around the globe.

Granting individuals the freedom to pursue their interests was not only prudent and rational for governments, it was essential to handle the required complexity of economic activity. To Smith, the function of government, with a few pragmatic exceptions, was to control force and fraud, and the free institutions of society were to take care of production, family, charity, and the rest of social life. Production simply would be more efficient if entrepreneurs and firms were free to respond creatively to public demands for goods and services, which would create great wealth for all nations that followed that course. There were two basic institutions, government and the market—the first based upon power and the second based upon free contract. Consequently, it was Smith who early saw the market as a separate social institution.

If most people followed their "natural sentiments," while the government provided rules for order, Smith considered this sufficient. If the rules of the government were fair, what took place under them could even be considered just. His was more a justice of practical means rather than a Platonic ideal requiring the actual achievement of fair results, however. As such, Smith's system does not satisfy many critics as a moral system at all. He considered it moral because it was practical. It produced wealth, which produced happiness. With Locke and Madison, he explicitly recognized that this prosperity would not be equally shared. Smith justified this by the general prosperity and social harmony it produced among all citizens, first in Britain and then worldwide. This practical good for society overall outweighed the fact that some might have some more and others somewhat less.[3]

The central institution of Locke's, Madison's, and Smith's systems — according to everyone from Marx to modern author Tom Bethel — was property. Bethel claimed that private property was the prime reason for the West's unique economic prosperity. Its success, especially relative to its main competitor, Islam, was due to their different views of how property should be owned. As early as Greece and Rome, greater legal and moral protections were given to property than in "barbarian" states. After the fall of Rome, literally every piece of property had to be defended in the chaos that followed. Rights to property and its inheritance in the West were hard-won from much weaker states than those that crushed it in the East, wrested in the former by the nobility, church, manors, guilds, and cities over centuries. When private property became more secure and morally and legally protected in the West in the Middle Ages, Europe finally began to outpace the Muslim world economically.[4] Classical author Victor Hanson even gave credit to private property ownership for the military superiority of the West as well. The freedom, independence, and cooperation ownership encouraged resulted in its more tenacious, imaginative, and technologically superior military institutions and the greater ability this gave them to prevail in arms over time.[5]

Why did the originally wealthier Muslim states not grow economically beyond a certain point? Islamic law had detailed rules for almost every aspect of life. As al Shafi'i noted, even when there was no rule, decisions must be derived from them. This was true for economic transactions as well, where detailed regulation of commerce was characteristic. As decisions accumulated, there was less flexibility to adapt to new conditions. Most important, Bethel argued, there was no moral right to private property under Islam, leaving all wealth under the control of the state. Property was basically distributed by the all-powerful Caliph or Sultan to his favorites and recalled to the state upon death. Bethel identified Muslim lands that were fruitful earlier becoming deserts because there was no incentive to care for property that could not be held for or transferred to future generations. Practically, why bother if it will all be taken away anyway?

Other cultures likewise recognized few private property rights. Bethel cited the greater survival rates of elephants under private property rules than under government protection in Africa as the most convincing evidence that, without property incentives, the practical effect was less efficient use of resources and environmental degradation. Most important, inheritance rights to property gave individuals, families, and communities independent power from the state that contributed to a general division of power in the society. Islam and most non-Western states never developed these independent centers as all power was granted to the state, all culminating at the top in the hands of a Sultan or king who designed and authorized everything. In feudalism, power was disbursed, even chaotic. Islam's property regime survived for 500 years under the Ottomans but the complexity of modern communication started to overwhelm its hierarchical system as early as the 18th century, and it broke down completely in the 20th.

Even within the West, property differences were important for economic development. The Anglo-American common law nations that emphasized practical private property protection tended to be more successful than the comprehensive continental European civil law systems that specified how property should be used—similar to the distinction Hayek labeled critical and constructive rationalism. In a modern review, *Wall Street Journal* columnist David Wessel was impressed that these long-ago legal decisions still affect the greater success of the practical U.S. and Britain with their larger stock markets, more shareholding citizens, and greater economic prosperity, as compared to the rest of Europe, as well as to how the West as a whole differed most economically from the remainder of the world.[6]

THE MARKET: MATHEMATICAL CONSTRUCTION
OR EVOLUTIONARY ORDER?

As we have seen, even Marx conceded that capitalism created an historically unique level of economic prosperity. The market rationalized all old social forms and produced greater wealth, more than all ages before combined. Yet, he also predicted that its markets would eventually fail. Marx based this conclusion on what he believed was a greater scientific understanding of the market than Smith. In volume one, section one, of his major work *Capital*, Marx offhandedly dismissed Smith's market as "subjective," as (at least partially) based upon what consumers subjectively desired.[7] Moreover, at least under capitalism, there was no such thing as "natural sentiments" for benevolence. It was all cash competition. If supply and demand were determined by people's sentiments rather than objective elements such as labor and capital, how could economics even be thought to be a science? A true science of economics required objectivity. So Marx followed the popular British economist, David Ricardo, who had expressed competition mathematically—fulfilling Marx's requirement for scientific objectivity.[8] Ricardo defined a true market as one with "perfect competition," that is as a market with many sellers and many buyers. Only under that objective condition of competition could a market work with true efficiency.

This definition was central to Marx because, when he found that there were not many sellers in the market of his day in the West, he concluded that something seriously wrong had developed under capitalism. Modern firms were consolidating into fewer and fewer monopolies, so he could predict scientifically from Ricardo's design that capitalism was failing. With fewer sellers, competition declined, wealth and power became more concentrated, fewer workers were required, and potential consumers became impoverished. This would necessarily lead to collapse and, finally, to a new socialist society where property was shared equally and everyone could prosper. Everything fit together with perfect logic.

Ricardo's mathematical definition of the market and Marx's popularization of it translated "perfect competition" into economic law around the world. This view of the market was so influential in the U.S. that it was enshrined by the Sherman Act of 1890 into the central component of American antitrust law. As a result, ever since, market law has set as its goal the maintenance of industry markets composed of many sellers or, more precisely—sometimes vigorously but often laconically—to keep one or a few companies from dominating any industry. While enforcement has been sporadic, a recent example was the government suit against software giant Microsoft. In Europe, this view was even more influential. In Germany, it is still illegal to have a "sale" on goods without the government's permission, which it grants infrequently and to all at the same time, perhaps twice a year, on the grounds that vigorous and frequent sales would unfairly undercut the prices of competitors and perhaps drive higher-cost companies out of business, upsetting the many-sellers requirement with this destructive competition.

Do you not see, argued the economist Joseph A. Schumpeter, destructive competition was the whole point of capitalism? Indeed, he defined the market as the process of "creative destruction."[9] While Marx recognized the destruction, his idea that there was a predetermined many buyers, many sellers form to the market led him to predict failure or success based upon whether that form was realized. To Schumpeter, there was no form to the market. It was simply the result of whatever happened as the result of free decisions made under its general rules. Whatever structure of buyers and sellers or customers resulted from these free choices was the efficient form for the market, without considering any particular form as "correct" or incorrect. Competition was not a mathematical number but what resulted when products were free to compete with each other. The proof of the market was what it delivered. Indeed, he argued that the most important type of competition was not even between existing firms in narrow industry markets like other wagonmakers but from new products like automobiles, not from other iron manufacturers but from substitutes like steel or aluminum, or from whole new industries never before conceived by adding machine or typewriter manufacturers like computers.

Unrestricted markets and the raw competition unleashed by them created whatever goods and services people wanted, and this success in meeting demand increased trade and created prosperity. Communism, democratic socialism, Islam, and other state systems tried to control this market chaos by creating governmental plans. Plans do order decisions to control the unpredictable. But this also makes it difficult to adapt to meet new circumstances inconsistent with or unexpected by the plan. Capitalism was creative by accepting new things because there was no prior planning of results, only preexisting general rules. This creativity was characteristic of capitalism, granting to it its dynamic nature that produced new ways and new wealth. Only governments that allowed great freedom within broad rules to guide producers did not frustrate innovation, change, and the prosperity that resulted from them.

This creative destruction in the West constantly swept away old things and ancient ways, which were constantly being replaced by new more efficient ones. Markets were constantly rationalized. Only governments could survive the assault because they were outside the market—a classic study of the survival of governmental units over time in the U.S. by political scientist Herbert Kaufman was titled, *Are Government Organizations Immortal?*[10] To a great extent they are. Their power is sufficient to survive market forces. Then, why could government not make firms immortal too? Generally, they have tried but have been unsuccessful, simply preserving inefficiency and increasingly fettering their markets. Private firms fail regularly, even more so since government protection has increased. In the U.S., with a vibrant market, hundreds of thousands of firms fail each year and are replaced by new ones. Freedom, thus, produces great wealth in a market, but it, not surprisingly, also produces great dissatisfaction from the old firms, institutions, and ways that are swept away by it.

In spite of this, whether for good or ill, the Schumpeterian view of the market as dynamic and unpredictable is eroding the Ricardoian one of stable markets and many buyers and sellers even in the U.S. In its recent Microsoft decision, the Federal appeals court rejected the Sherman view that monopoly power "may be inferred from the predominant share of the market" alone. Instead, it held that "the possibility of new entrants" and substitute products into the market must be considered in any charge of monopoly power against private firms by the government, endorsing the proposition of a market of creation and destruction that will produce ever more wealth.[11]

MARKET FAIRNESS: THE RULE OF LAW

Still, market freedom has its limits. As Nobel economist Hayek argued, there simply is no such thing as laissez faire—a market with no government—in the real world.[12] Real markets are free only within "rules of the game." Western markets like Britain and the U.S. use broader rules and more freedom, but their governments still must create rules or there is no guide for businessmen or judges to follow in settling commercial disputes. Coercion and fraud must be declared as illicit, and this is done by government. There must be rules to establish what property rights mean, what cannot be contracted (e.g., slavery), when contracts are broken or property infringed, and how they are to be adjudicated. Following Locke, government must set known and indiscriminate rules within which free economic life can prosper. While fewer rules make it easier for citizens to know the law, so they may obey it, and make it easier for government to administer, there must be some rules of law. The essential quality of these rules, from Locke to Hayek, is that all are treated fairly and equally under them.

Yet many, following Plato, insist that fair rules by themselves are insufficient. The results must be fair too, driving the question once again back to basic matters. Locke and Madison argue that predetermined results are inconsistent with freedom and, therefore, that fair rules are as far as one should go. As long as the rules do not favor one group or interest above another, that is all that is required. Fair rules only need to apply equally to all, as in baseball. Applying a single fair standard to all equally is usually called "the rule of law." It is a difficult standard to meet. Most nations at most times create special provisions advantaging particular nationalities, classes, interests, religions, genders, ages, and groups because they are viewed as especially needy or valued. A rule of law can only exist if people can restrain themselves from giving special advantages to some groups over others, primarily their own groups and interests over others. For this, a tradition of self-restraint is critical, as history has shown according to Hayek and others, primarily from some religious tradition. Honesty, fair play, trust, lawfulness, respect for others' property, responsibility for oneself and others, and moderation in making demands on government are all required.

Hayek argued that two values are the most important to develop a tradition of self-restraint that promotes freedom and markets, support for the family and for several property.[13] Islam, Judaism, Buddhism, Hinduism, The People, and others have supported the family, and this has allowed them to survive and prosper over time. But support for both several property and the family has been rare, basically confined to Greece and early Rome and transferred throughout Europe during its feudal reconstruction after the empire's fall, and then to their colonies in the newly discovered worlds of West and South. In recent years, rule of law in this sense has also been successfully transferred to Buddhist-influenced regimes in Asia such as Japan, Taiwan, Singapore, Hong Kong, and some others. But it remains rather exceptional. Even in the West—including the U.S.—Hayek finds that its democratic governments find it increasingly difficult to resist group and interest pressures for special exceptions and preferences, compromising the strength of their own rules of law and the prosperity that results from them.

DOES THE MARKET WORK—
AT LEAST IN PRODUCING WEALTH?

Marx predicted that, in the end, free market capitalism would lead to impoverishment. At least so far, there is little evidence of this, although perhaps not enough time has elapsed for it to come true. Rather, market or capitalist economic freedom is very highly correlated with both societal and per capita wealth. Moreover, the relationship has been consistent over a significant period of time, as is convincingly demonstrated by World Bank data, presented in the *Index of Economic Freedom*.[14] Interestingly, the most economically free markets were not in Western Europe or the United States, but Hong Kong and Singapore, although both were former British colonies, as was Bahrain the fourth most economically free. Still, 10 of the top 14 most economically free nations were Western—defined as a country that is European or a European former colony in the Western hemisphere, or in Austral-Asia—and all also ranked among the world's wealthiest countries. The U.S. was tied for fourth on economic freedom and was second highest on wealth per person worldwide. Western nations also represented 46 of the 66 next most economically free markets and they too were generally wealthier. Only nine Western markets were rated economically unfree, and all of these were formerly forcibly part of the now-departed Soviet Union and were also found to be much less wealthy.

Other data suggest that political freedom is even more uniquely Western than economic freedom and is just as highly correlated with economic prosperity. The results, as presented by the bipartisan—one of its founders was Eleanor Roosevelt—and well-respected Freedom House, are remarkable.[15] All of the most-free nations (1.0 on the Freedom House scale) are Western, naturally including the U.S. Most of the next most free (1.5 score) are Western too, with Japan, Taiwan, and South Africa also qualifying as highly free nations. These nations also tend to be among the world's wealthiest. The only Western nation not politically free at all in the study was hardly following the Western model, since it was the communist nation Cuba, which is also very poor. Only 29 of the world's 217 countries rate the most-free ranking, representing a small fraction of the globe's population. Only slightly more than one-third of the world's population even qualifies for Freedom House' looser definition of political freedom.

Surprisingly, the amount of democracy in a nation does not correlate with wealth at all and is only weakly related to political freedom. Much more important than voting or democratic participation or how highly educated is the population in explaining wealth is whether a nation has a strong rule of law. This seems particularly important for developing nations, where too much democracy seems even to hold a nation back from prosperity (as Aristotle had predicted).[16] As Locke and Hayek expected, the World Bank data demonstrate what is important for prosperity is rule of law. It seems as if rule of law is required first, to provide legitimate order and security of property, which in turn can allow political freedom, which is favorable to economic freedom and the development of markets, which leads to prosperity. Only a few nations, 29 in number, have been able to follow this path to success, the most successful on all of these measures together—on rule of law, political freedom, market freedom, and wealth combined—being the United States.

Is the market, then, the ideal system—because it produces the greatest wealth and freedom, as many capitalists would argue? Well, there was that disastrous market failure of the 1930s Great Depression. Could there be another one? Japan and Europe are already stagnant in economic growth and even the U.S. rate might be slowing. Additionally, many people in the West clearly fall behind and live in poverty. Does the fact that there are millions of poor in the West mean that it is not just, as Plato would undoubtedly conclude? Does this at least justify intervening in the market to favor the disadvantaged, as many progressives would argue? Or would special laws for sympathetic groups multiply and undermine the rule of law, as Hayek feared might be the case? Or will this intervention simply fetter the market and make it less free and productive, as Schumpeter predicted? But, if this is so, why with all of the regulation of the post New Deal era has the U.S. still been the most prosperous nation? Or is the party almost over?

Even if it is true that the market is the most efficient way to produce wealth for all, are there not other values higher than efficiency and material ease? What does the capitalist emphasis upon the "cash nexus," materialism, consumerism, hyper-rationality, and unrestricted freedom do to human social and moral life?

NOTES

1. John Locke, *Second Treatise on Government*, in Ernest Barker, ed., *Social Contract* (New York: Oxford University Press, 1962).

2. *The Federalist Papers*, No. 10.

3. Adam Smith, *An Inquiry into the Nature and Causes of the Wealth of Nations* (New York: The Modern Library, 1937). Also see Donald Devine, "Adam Smith and the Problem of Justice in Capitalist Society," *Journal of Legal Studies* (June 1977), 399–409. Smith never full resolved the distinction between the natural and market prices but, in any event, the natural price had no "objective" norm that "should" be achieved for a market to "work"; see James M. Buchanan, *Cost and Choice* (Chicago: Markham, 1969), 3. For the pencil example, see Leonard E. Read, *I, Pencil* (Irvington-on-Hudson, N.Y.: Foundation for Economic Education).

4. Tom Bethell, *The Noblest Triumph: Property and Prosperity Through the Ages* (New York: Palgrave, 1998), 230–42 and 285–89. For a Muslim confirmation, see Maalouf, 263. Also see Victor Davis Hanson, *The Other Greeks* (New York: Free Press, 1995).

5. Victor Davis Hanson, *Carnage and Culture* (New York: Doubleday, 2001), especially 441–44.

6. David Wessel, "The Legal DNA of Good Economies," *The Wall Street Journal,* 6 September 2001, A1.

7. Karl Marx, *Capital*, trans. Ben Fowkes (New York: Penguin Classics, 1992), Vol. I, Ch. 1.

8. Joseph A. Schumpeter, "Marx the Economist," in *Capitalism, Socialism and Democracy* (New York: Harper and Row, 1950), 3.

9. Joseph A. Schumpeter, "Process of Creative Destruction," in *Capitalism, Socialism and Democracy* (New York: Harper and Row, 1950), 7.

10. Herbert Kaufman, *Are Government Organizations Immortal?* (Washington, D.C.: The Brookings Institution, 1976).

11. *U.S. v. Microsoft*, 253 F. 3rd. 34: 20.

12. F. A. Hayek, "Economic Policy and Rule of Law," chap. 15 in *The Constitution of Liberty* (Chicago: University of Chicago Press, 1960).

13. F. A. Hayek, *The Fatal Conceit* (Chicago: University of Chicago Press, 1988), 137.

14. Gerald P. O'Driscoll, Jr., Kim Holmes, and Melanie Kirkpatrick, *2000 Index of Economic Freedom* (Washington, D.C.: The Heritage Foundation and Dow Jones & Co., Inc., 2000), including table on Economic Freedom and Wealth, based upon World Bank data.

15. Freedom House, "Combined Average Ratings," in *Freedom in the World* (New York: Freedom House, 2001), 660–61.

16. David Dollar and Aart Kraay, "Democracy and Rule of Law in Supporting Economic Growth," in *Property Rights, Political Rights and the Development of Poor Countries in the Post-Colonial World*, <http://www.worldbank.org/research/growth>. Also see Robert J. Barro, "Rule of Law, Democracy and Economic Performance," in O'Driscoll, *et al.*, *2000 Index of Economic Freedom*, 31–50.

Chapter Eight

Market and Democratic Decay

CRISIS OF THE FAMILY AND SOCIAL ORDER?

Western values in general and American institutions in particular have demonstrated many advantages over alternative world approaches, especially in producing freedom and economic prosperity. That very freedom, however, has been criticized as likely leading to licentiousness, excess, lawlessness, and disorder. This license and the immorality that it believes results from it is fundamentalist Islam's major indictment against the West and of the United States in particular. Even many in America today believe its democracy and market are in serious decline and even in decay as a result of slipping moral standards. Charges of corruption in government and financial fraud in the market appear in the news each day. To many, the greatest threat is to the most fundamental social institution, the family and the community life it sustains, upon whose support rests the health of both its market and its government.

Let us begin with three of America's particular friends. Former Senator Daniel Patrick Moynihan, columnist Charles Krauthammer, and social scientist Robert Putnam. All tend to agree that the market and its democratic government have produced great riches for most Americans, but they also document a significant decline in social life today that has accompanied this prosperity. While starting from a detached and scientific evaluation of American social behavior, Senator Moynihan concludes from his observations that "we are getting used to a lot of behavior that is not good for us." While things go "upwards and downwards," there recently has been "a manifest decline of the American civic order." Indeed, today, "the amount of deviant behavior in American society has increased beyond the levels the community can 'afford to recognize.'" So, deviancy has been redefined down "to exempt much conduct previously stigmatized" and to consider what was once thought abnormal as normal.[1] Specifically, there has been an "earthquake" in the family that has caused very high levels of illegitimacy and lower levels of care for and protection of children. The decline in two-parent families has directly led to poorer health for these children and lower quality education for them. To him, traditional families are the "clear" solution to poverty, and even crime is best controlled when boys have resident fathers in an intact family setting.

The facts of this decline and the social disorder it caused are clear. Yet, the people—or, more properly, he refers to democratic leaders and opinion makers rather than average middle class citizens—do not seem able to come to grips with the problem and so ignore it. They "define deviancy down" and call what used to be considered deviant behavior—illegitimate birth, the decline of marriage, mental illness, and high levels of violent crime—normal. That way, they can avoid facing the problem. If deviance becomes too widespread, apparently, democratic leaders cannot "afford" to recognize too many people as deviants—for, after all, they can vote against them. This process of normalization of aberrant behavior, however, is at "some peril" to the survival of the good society because the actual problems persist. The crisis of the family and society are real and profound in their effects and probably will continue to degenerate, especially if they must be ignored because many will not or cannot accept the reality.

Former psychologist Krauthammer says it is worse than that. There are actually two mental strategies—denial and distraction. Moynihan is correct regarding denial but the other strategy is just as destructive. Psychological distraction directs the blame for unpleasant realities away from the true cause to a scapegoat, in the case of the decline of values in America, to the middle class, whose behavior is made to look as or more perverse than the behavior they criticize as deviant. Opinion makers and intellectuals generally tend to see middle class morality as fake and wrong. So, they created a "phony" morality for the middle classes that exaggerates their failings and claims those are just as bad as illegitimacy, maltreated children, and crime. Their strategy is to distract the middle class and the political power they wield from taking action to control the truly deviant behavior. Rather than expressing concern for the real deviancy, opinion makers invent problems: fantasy "child abuse"—two-thirds of which allegations were ultimately dismissed outright; or "date rape" against young women—73% of whom told interviewers they did not consider themselves raped; or "thought crimes" of white citizens for not being "tolerant" enough of minority groups. Thus, both denial and distraction ignore real problems like real child abuse, rape, and violent crime, and inhibit their ability to be resolved.[2]

Whatever the precise nature or cause of the problem, both authors give strong evidence that the number one social institution, the family, is in serious decline in America today. Putnam goes even further. He systematically investigated the whole voluntary and local Tocquevillean social order that has been characteristic of America until recent times to determine its health. He concluded that this local community life has seriously eroded in the U.S. during the later years of the 20th century, after a large upsurge in the late 19th and early 20th centuries.[3] As a result of his extensive study of many forms of associational records and related social research, he demonstrates that voluntary social activity of all types has declined significantly in recent years. Democratic participation in voting and campaigning, volunteering for charitable causes, and even community social life such as bowling and visiting neighbors is declining in terms of the number of people engaged in these societal-building activities. Civic life is eroding along with the family, and he wonders whether this only affects the U.S. or is universal, coming to affect other nations too?

Krauthammer the psychologist and Moynihan the former social science professor try to use neutral, scientific-sounding verbiage to avoid the language of morality and values. Yet, interestingly, there is a moral urgency to both of their critiques—they are almost pleading for help for the family behind the sterile words. It is clear the authors think denial and distortion are wrong in a moral sense and Krauthammer specifically condemns both strategies as moral equivalence. Of course, not all view this as a problem to be remedied: some critics accept unconventional or individualistic lifestyles as truly morally equivalent or even superior to the traditional family. Krauthammer, who has become a conservative, in fact blames this alternative ideology for devising and utilizing the strategy of distortion as a political weapon. They charge the tongue-tied middle class majority with phony crimes, say they are intolerant or even just unreasonable, and intimidate this easy target, who will not or cannot fight back to defend their traditional values.

The more interesting charge is from the liberal, Moynihan. To him, the major measures of social decline—the increase in welfare dependency, higher medical pathology for children, the decline in educational proficiency, and more crime—have one source: the decline in intact, two-parent families. Where families are strong, there is no decline; where families are weak, the decline is real. Yet, with more and more divorce and single-parent families, what politician can afford to mention the problem, much less mobilize to solve it? He is upset that "there is money to be made out of bad schools," that textbooks promote that "divorce represents part of the normal family life cycle," that marriage "cannot provide a secure or permanent status" for heterosexuals, and that homosexual, bisexual, commune/group marriage, single parenthood, and living together are equivalent to marriage as just another "lifestyle choice." This is not maintaining neutrality, but it is a moral choice

that makes the previously deviant lifestyles morally equivalent to marriage—
even if that happens to lead to less protection for children. If illegitimacy, divorce, welfare dependency, and crime are real problems, is the solution not
obvious that the way to deal with them is simply to mobilize the moral
courage necessary to rebuild the traditional family?

IS THE WHOLE WEST SUFFERING FROM
INEVITABLE SOCIAL DECAY?

The belief that there is social decline in the West generally is very widespread
but many influential voices have been raised against the traditional family.
Plato claimed that the bourgeois two-parent family was morally corrupt by its
very nature because it tried to advantage one's own children over the rest of
the community. Nietzsche specifically cited conventional Western morality,
including its value of family obligation, as the cause of its social decay. The
Western idea of moral responsibility pulled down the morally superior individual, the superman, to the level of commonness in conventional community
and family duty. With Emerson, Thoreau, Camus, and many other individualists, he took the position that true morality required that one should always
follow one's own star, rationally, rather than be restricted by traditional moral
norms or values, especially not to sacrifice one's genius and creativity to the
restrictive demands of mundane family obligation.

Even individualists who do support traditional morality and the family
make high demands of them if they are not to become corrupt. Entrepreneur
Andrew Carnegie agreed that the creative individual would go to the top in a
competitive market, while moral fitness did not necessarily assure who would
be at the top or bottom. The resulting inequality in wealth under a free market would almost inevitably lead to inequalities and injustices to the least
clever in society, which would naturally result in social decay, at least for
them. But there was a Christian moral obligation against nature to help those
who cannot compete as effectively. Voluntary charity was required from all
who are more favored by merit in the market's competitive process if its system is to be just or even survive over time, as Smith himself had observed.
Indeed, Carnegie argued that people of great wealth have the greatest individual obligation to give away a great part of their wealth to the poor. Any
"man who dies thus rich thus dies disgraced." If the rich do not give to the
poor, all free social institutions, including the family, will weaken and people
will look for socialistic solutions or worse. The very survival of the productive capitalist system depends utterly upon the individual moral choice of the
wealthy to give away much of their fortunes.[4]

Some chance, retorted Marx: cash rules the capitalist world and most everyone in it. In fact, unlike Carnegie, very few rich men give their wealth away
and never will. They hoard it for themselves and their children. Not only do
capitalists not give their money away, most successfully lobby for additional
funds or benefits from the government. Social forces are what count anyway,
not individual moral sentiments. Large matters such as the survival of capitalism or of the family are not individual moral problems but are determined by
great historical processes and forces. Market rationality does create more
wealth, but that increased understanding of how markets operate concentrates
wealth over time at the top, as even Carnegie admits. This provokes reaction
from the impoverished workers who form unions, then political parties and,
when a few rich men and intellectuals join, will prevail and overthrow capitalism. The economic forces, the cash "nexus," especially corrupts the family
under the later stages of capitalism. Only proceeding to the following stage of
communism can create a healthy society. What the critics see in the U.S. today
is the inevitable decay of capitalism that will only accelerate over time. Only
after destroying the cause of conflict—the unequal distribution of property—
will what are now called family relations become happy ones for all peoples.

Even de Tocqueville, who supported bourgeois, even Christian family values and Western views of property, freedom, and limited government, agreed
with Marx that historical forces were working to undermine those values. The
rising worldwide desire for equality meant more political power would be put
in the hands of the people, which would lead them to demand that governments "secure their gratifications and to watch over their fate." No one will
be able to resist the voice of the people, whose rule would be "absolute,
minute, regular, provident and mild," overriding any divisions or limitations
placed upon it. Great fortunes would be swept away to fund this welfare state
so that no independent leadership could stand against the populist tide. Individual responsibility could only survive if the overwhelming percentage of
the people paid their own way and had independent power guaranteed by
strong property rights. But most people would rather pursue their daily "petty
pleasures," and democratic leaders would indulge them in their ways, not dar-
ing to correct them but providing more and more free benefits.[5] The French
aristocrat would not be surprised that a seemingly powerful Senator like
Moynihan only wrote his critique of public morality for a small-circulation
academic magazine that the average person would not see—or that he felt
pressured to vote against the welfare-limiting provisions of the Welfare Reform Act of 1996. In the end, concluded de Tocqueville, government welfare
would so weaken their character that the people, in moral decline, would become unfit for freedom—although the resulting despotism would be mild
enough even to escape most people's notice.

The economic historian Schumpeter also agreed that decline was likely, but Marx was wrong about the cause. Looking at the facts one had to conclude that capitalism led to widespread prosperity, not impoverishment. This prosperity, however, would not lead to popular satisfaction but would provoke an enormous dissatisfaction with capitalism that would be equally fatal to its continued survival. Indeed, from Plato's Athens to imperial Rome to the split of the Western church to the break-up of colonialism, decline has been more associated with increasing material prosperity and luxury than with declining economic conditions. Those without wealth always want more, and the political leaders will not stand in their way, especially in a democracy. The wealthy and powerful would like to preserve capitalism, but its leaders are reluctant to take heroic moral stands, which were characteristic of feudal rather than business thinking. Capitalism encourages a calculating attitude, not a courageous one. A businessman dares not confront an intellectual for fear of looking unprofessional or ignorant. Capitalism rewards businessmen with profits when they satisfy popular demands, not when they decide what is good for people. So democratic capitalism cannot even rally to save its own civilization—which only survived as long as it did because the landed, feudal aristocracy—hereditary in Europe or Adams' natural aristocracy in the U.S.— thought it was its duty to preserve society.

It was only the West's old fashioned, even feudal values like duty that kept the government and society in order so that the capitalists could produce and become rich. But the capitalists and the intellectuals they created to provide the brains to drive the business system deride their old fashioned protectors as rubes, provincials, puritans, moralistic, WASPs, nerds, and spoilsports, undermining the only political authorities that could support the businessmen in their affluence. After ridiculing their staid morality and taxing away their hereditary property in the name of greater economic efficiency, there is no one left who will stand against the tide and defend property, feudal or capitalist. Schumpeter's most interesting conclusion is that capitalism may not even have been the unique form of social organization that Marx said it was— capitalism may merely be the final stage of feudalism. Without the "protecting strata" of the old aristocratic classes and the moral justification for their rule that they—together with the equally ridiculed clergy—provided, no one has the necessary legitimacy to govern under capitalism. So, with the people not having trusted leaders any longer, democratic politicians increasingly "fetter" capitalism in an attempt to satisfy the masses, and the market becomes more and more irrational and inefficient.

Finally, the supporting values of capitalism—the family, children, duty, religion, community, and association—are whittled away by its calculating, bookkeeping mentality of self-interest first. When people finally calculate that children are an economic drag under capitalism, requiring scores of years of expensive investment in nurturing and education before becoming productive —unlike on the farm where their labor is an early and inexpensive economic benefit—the moral commandment "to increase and multiply" is undermined, and the family will disintegrate. So will the whole driving force of capitalism, which always assumed that the individual must work hard so he could support his family for its motivation. Without the obligations, why work long or even full time? Powerful but illegitimate government, fettered markets, diminished desire to work, and the decay of family and duty inevitably lead to decline.[6] Western civilization will simply collapse into the soft democratic egalitarianism and mild authoritarianism that de Tocqueville predicted for it so many years before.

CAN THE DECAY BE REVERSED?

Is decay inevitable? Social critic Lewis Lehrman argues that the decay is simply the result of a decline in individual morality and can be reversed by a return to traditional values. Schumpeter may write in terms of impersonal social forces but when one strips away the imagery, he simply is saying that the West abandoned the values of feudal Christianity that created it.[7] Lehrman does not oppose the market; he calls it the "least imperfect" economic system. But market freedom needs a social and moral order to sustain it, as most of its theorists and supporters recognize. Without morality, the market, government, family, and society must decline. It does not even take a majority to pull the whole system down. Not only must the political class support the old values, as Schumpeter argued, but "every soul" must be moral for a healthy society. As Locke taught, the problem does come down to individual morality. A people without moral values will not even know how to identify what are "fair" market or democratic rules. These are not abstractions but both depend upon how human beings think and act about morality. In the United States the only concrete morality possible is that of Judeo-based Christianity. Rather than rely upon the old morality, the only other solution is to pass more laws and hire more regulators to force people to obey them. Yet, if the people are not virtuous, society will require an "armed camp of police" to keep the peace, and freedom cannot survive. If the people turn back to their historical morality, however, social decay can be reversed and a healthy family and a free society can still be enjoyed.[8]

Oh, that it could be so simple, concludes modern author George Ritzer, speaking for many others: increased morality is not sufficient to reverse the decline. In a very popular article, he claims that even if everyone was moral individually, large social forces would push them to act against what they thought was personally right, even in ways that may not be rational for them. Today, globalization overwhelms individual morality in ways that now cannot even be controlled by any one national government. Markets are worldwide and national laws cannot reach the sources of the problems. Ritzer made the McDonalds hamburger chain the archetype for the new reality. McDonalds rationalizes food production worldwide with such efficiency, predictability, calculation, technology, and control that individuals are reduced "to acting like robots." The "mystery and excitement" are removed from mealtime, and cholesterol, pesticides, and artificial ingredients are added to it in ways that threaten world health. Even if government could be mobilized to counteract its attraction, no one nation controls McDonald's global network. The pursuit of worldwide rational efficiency by business becomes the "irrationality of rationality" for the individuals affected by it. People are attracted by the rationally researched and, consequently, nice-tasting food but get hardening of the arteries as the result. The solution is not more individual morality but more "control" over irrational market rationalization.[9]

Government is the only possible solution to achieve that control. The great social theorist of the modern welfare state, Gunnar Myrdal, argued that a Lockean or Smithean capitalism based upon a natural harmony between individual interests and the common good was simply mythical. Rather, market freedom leads to disorder. The reason government regulation does not work is because it is based upon political whim and popular passion. The solution is not no government control, as the free marketers would like, but expert government planning. Only planning can rationalize markets, using reason rather than politics or blind market forces. In fact, rational planning has been slowly evolving over time in the West. Starting in Europe and transferred to the U.S. by professor and future president Woodrow Wilson in the early 20th century, the old unfettered market and divided government were declared inadequate to meet the challenges of modern life. Wilson specifically criticized the separation of powers as frustrating the government's ability to act on the national scale necessary to solve the dislocations and called for centralization of power in the presidency so that it could act positively to promote societal welfare. Wilson created the Federal Reserve in 1913 to rationalize the central mechanism of capitalism, the banks; the Clinton Antitrust Act bureaucracy at the Department of Justice and the Federal Trade Commission to regulate commerce in 1914; and the farm loan program to manage the largest industry, agriculture, in 1916.[10] While he enacted the early reforms, it was not until the Great Depression of the 1930s undermined support for the old institutions that President Franklin Roosevelt was able to extend rational welfare state planning to the remainder of the economy.

So why has planning not yet rationalized the market? To some extent, it is the global reach of trade, but the real problem is that the very people concerned about the social decay are reluctant to give up enough power to the experts to do the necessary planning to control it. Myrdal was concerned even in 1964 that planning and the welfare state had a negative connotation because people thought that planning would take away their freedom. Instead, people had to be convinced that more logical and comprehensive planning would simply allow them to enjoy their freedom more positively and rationally. Then, they might be willing to concede the needed power to democratic experts.[11] Until then, economic irrationality and social decay were inevitable. The new welfare state did lead to more planning, but politicians too often turned the law into what the jurist Frederic Bastiat called "legal plunder" rather than rationalizing the process. Plunder was the result of human greed, which was probably inherent in human nature, and the "false philanthropy" of government planning, which simply did not work, he argued. No expert has any idea how to reverse social decay nor how to allocate resources rationally without relying upon a market. The solution to social decay was getting government, which Bastiat believed created many of the problems, out of the way and allow individuals and families the freedom to solve the problems themselves.[12]

THERE IS ONE CLEAR SOLUTION?

Again, to much of the world, that freedom is itself the problem. Islam, especially, finds that there is just one cause of the West's and America's family and social decay, and that is not following God's law. The West has lost whatever moral authority or even belief it possessed earlier and today is in inevitable decay and decline, as even secular pro-Westerners like Schumpeter understood. In plain terms, the West has lost its Christian values, and it cannot retain a moral and healthy family or society without them for very long. Indeed, the West really needs an even stronger religion like Islam. The church-state, community-government separation is probably an inherent flaw in Christianity, for a truly moral society requires a unification of government and morality, as Rousseau made so evident. Christian history in the West proves that its idea of freedom leads to license and decay. It is difficult to believe that a simple chain of hamburger restaurants cannot be overcome by sufficient moral and political commitment. Islam's solution to the problem of market rationalization is to fight it. It does this by enforcing submission to the law of Shari'a and promising that the resulting moral order—including that of the family—will be strong and protective of all, especially of children.

There is good reason to believe that Muslims will win by default. While the Western family is disintegrating, United Nations population data demonstrate that Islam's strong families are producing more than enough children to double its followers, while the West is not replacing itself.[13] Islam's solution is to overtake Christianity's population before the West understands what is happening.

WELL, IS IT INDIVIDUAL RESPONSIBILITY OR SELF-RELIANCE?

Do human beings have some duty to neighbor or community or government? and if so, what is the basis of that obligation? Or are Nietzsche, Emerson, and Thoreau correct—is one's only responsibility to oneself, to do whatever he or she individually thinks is right? What do you think? While it might not be socially acceptable to say that your own self-interest is your only guide, is that actually the way people think and act? What would you do with Gyges' ring? In reality, in private, is it not a bit cool to say: "I do my own thing." Or "It all depends" (on what I feel), which is pretty much the same thing? Who says authoritatively that an individual must be responsible, and to what or whom? Isn't doing one's own thing the real morality today?

On the other hand:

1. *How do you operate in your own life? Do you feel some obligation to your children or spouse or should your own comfort come first?*
2. *How about outside the home? As a mother or father or friend, do you teach selfishness or indifference to the suffering of others to your own or others' children as something to emulate? Should they be neutral toward other people's suffering or not? Does it matter if inflicting pain seems no better to them than helping people—or not? Why, who says so? If you just feel it, what if I do not?*
3. *How do you think about the NYC firefighters in the Twin Towers rescue— do you respect them or think they were foolhardy? Would you teach your children that duty is good or irrational behavior? Why does heroic behavior tend to be respected? Does it matter whether it is or not? Should children be taught neutrality about such actions?*
4. *The steelworkers who cleared the debris where the Twin Towers stood were cheered—even by the cynical media—why? Is even everyday work sometimes heroic and worthy? Is everyone important for society to be successful, as Lehrman argued? Should individual heroic action be encouraged, discouraged, or does it make no difference? Why?*

5. *Why do religious leaders always show up among the most respected Americans; certainly they are not the most glamorous or wealthy or powerful? They even get caught in scandals. Should the professions Schumpeter mentioned as heroic—warrior, protector, national leader, local notables and officials, craftsmen, clergy—be taught to be respected? Or is that just "boosterism" or myth?*

6. *How about in the government? Do neutral experts solve the problems in the community or government, or does nothing happen unless some individual moral decision is made first? Experts certainly make many decisions, but whatever one thinks of the reforms, it took Newt Gingrich's moralistic commitment to welfare reform and Rudy Gulianni's to locking up miscreants, both of which Moynihan opposed, to produce some new ideas and action on the problems the Senator himself thought needed solution. Both of his political opponents made moral choices (right or wrong) that family responsibility was preferable to welfare dependency or that even minor laws against street crime had to be enforced, and they acted on these moral beliefs with some dramatic social consequences. Some evidence even suggests they might have started matters "up," again, as Moynihan hoped.*

7. *Does it all depend? Is all behavior equally correct? Is Material Madonna equal to Christ's Madonna? Is Brittany Spears better than Mother Teresa, or vice versa? Are Jimmy Carter and Osama bin Laden the same? Who or what says so or says not?*

IF THERE IS RESPONSIBILITY, IS IT THE GOVERNMENT'S, THE MARKET'S, OR ONE'S OWN?

If there is a moral responsibility, is the duty individual or collective? If it is individual, how should he or she meet that obligation? If it is collective, should it be accomplished through voluntary groups, or is the government the proper means, and at what level—national, regional, or local—or with what mix? Clearly, if market rationalization or other outside forces are the cause, individuals alone cannot effectively resist them. Only some equally great or greater counter-force can offset them. Usually, only government or even international government is thought to have the necessary power to counteract such amoral forces. Consequently, whether the cause is moral or from objective forces, government—and its obligations and responsibilities, if any—must be considered.

While comprehensive governmental solutions are currently in some disfavor because of the fall of communism and due to the inequities that still persist in the West after more than a century of welfare state planning, many people—probably a majority—still look to government for solutions, even in the "capitalist" U.S. Pure libertarianism receives a miniscule percentage of the popular vote there, and even under Ronald Reagan, only a few government programs were privatized, de-federalized, or even outsourced to private firms. Perhaps socialism is even still the leading idea in the West. European leaders are certainly building a market even more regulated by experts and with less popular participation—even though this centralized European Union and common Euro market has provoked significant popular opposition. While the stagflation of the Jimmy Carter presidency and the fact that even Democratic presidential candidates have denied they have supported big government thereafter suggests that the planned welfare state is weakened, it is still the predominant characteristic of American government. National government still consumes about 20 percent of national income in the U.S. and controls most of the rest through regulation of some sort or another. Property rights are often trumped by environmental, health, and labor regulations, usually without requiring compensation for any restrictions on property use. With government even more popular as a solution in the rest of the world, one cannot ignore the fact that the state is the dominant solution.

Even the American Founders did not oppose government, but only wanted to limit it. They demanded freedom because people could be virtuous, but total freedom could only be the answer if humans were always angels. They were not. So they limited freedom by rules of law that could only be devised by governments, local and national. But they cited history that governments do bad things too, so they also limited its power in many ways, especially by dividing it. Modern history has confirmed their suspicions. Hitler's and Stalin's governments killed more of their own peoples domestically than were killed in the two world wars combined. Even democracies—and, of, course, Hitler was elected—do plunder and can weaken their people by promising free lunches, as not only de Tocqueville but Aristotle and Cicero also warned.[14] The Founders relied upon freedom for most of social life and, at least for a time, Smith's invisible hand, energized by self-interest and Locke's long-term self-interest to get to Heaven seemed to work at least in providing material well being. Yet, why should government not grow further than they thought necessary to let expert planning solve the remaining inequities, as Myrdal and most moderns demand? Or is Schumpeter correct that planning fetters the market further and leads to a call for total planning, the end of capitalism, and maybe of democracy too?

Can and should government solve the problems of social decay? Let us consider further.

1. *The planned welfare state has existed in Europe and the United States for almost a century. Has it solved the problems of health, welfare, and education it promised? If it has not, what is there that gives hope that it will succeed sometime in the future? Is not some more comprehensive solution like Plato's Republic or Marx's communism necessary to really solve them?*

2. *Or is relying upon government simply a weakness, an inability to rely upon self, as Emerson and Thoreau suggested? Is it a natural weakness to look to a father-substitute to solve all our problems"? Or is the hope for compassionate government a weakness particular to Western culture, as Nietzsche suggested—is it a Santa Claus complex embedded in the civilization? Or is it just normal human behavior to find someone else to solve one's problems?*

3. *With government's record in the 20th century, killing more of its own peoples than did war, is it even rational to trust it with the power to plan all of social life?*

4. *Even in the United States, does the record of the government solving even simple problems justify trust? On March 18, 1994, the Postal Service in Chicago was discovered with 200 pounds of mail burning in a poor neighborhood and, when forced to check further, found 20,000 more undelivered pieces dating back to the 1970s. Is there more out there somewhere?*

5. *What about the rationality of overall market regulation? Banks were viewed as the central market institutions both when the Federal Reserve System was created in 1913 and when general market regulation started in the 1930s, at times banks did most of the lending. Yet, bank lending was down to 40 percent of total investment by the 1970s, and is below 20 percent today. Why is the regulatory structure hardly changed?*

6. *Why do small businesses produce all of the net new jobs, but they tend to escape the helpful protecting arms of the regulators? Yet, when regulators notice them, they can be very "effective": the EPA eliminated 40 percent of gas stations in the 1990s, presumably to stop oil leaks into the ground—primarily mom and pop stations—leaving mostly national chains today.*

7. *What about the basic government function, even to Smith, of handling communicable diseases? In 1999, the FDA speculated that mercury traces in DTP (diphtheria, tetanus, and pertussis [whooping cough]) vaccines might be dangerous and asked the National Academy of Science to look at the problem. NAS concluded there was no evidence that mercury in vaccines caused harm but still, for some reason (probably environmentalist political pressure) advised the traces should be removed*

anyway. By 2001, there was a month back-order delay for the government vaccination program that was supposed to perform 60 percent of children's vaccinations. This for a disease (diphtheria) that in 1920 struck 206,939 children and killed from 10 to 20 percent of them. Should the same FDA also handle anthrax outbreaks?

8. *The two biggest programs, considered the welfare state's greatest successes—Social Security and Medicare—are both slated by government data to go bankrupt in 30 years or less. Both are expected to begin paying out more funds than they take in as early as 2016. Any attempt to rationalize them is greeted by claims that reformers are trying to hurt seniors and spending increases further. Does this not make reform impossible and guarantee bankruptcy sooner or later?*

9. *The front line troops of the welfare state, the National Association of Social Workers (143,000 strong) voted in August 1993 not to take a stand on the moral status of suicide but would remain neutral about it. They said people should consider suicide an option if a patient wanted to kill himself (no matter what his or her mental condition?) but that it "probably" would be unethical for a social worker to directly assist a person in killing himself.*

10. *Does government make any difference? Government data show that drastically increased government welfare spending did not result in higher, healthier birthweights for infants in the U.S. over this period—even with large increases in societal wealth and health generally. Likewise, the percentage of children born to unmarried parents—the problem that so distressed Moynihan—skyrocketed up and continued after welfare reform. Does this failure after spending so much time and so many resources undermine the whole idea of a welfare state? Or is more money the solution? How much more?*

11. *Of course, the middle class has done extraordinarily well during this period, and more people have been added to its ranks. The market obviously helps the middle class. The justification for government welfare, however, is to assist those not helped by the market, supposedly because it is the morally or socially right thing to do. Is this so? The biggest government welfare programs like Social Security and Medicare are actually aimed at the middle class. Is Marx correct that capitalist government just aids the ruling classes? Or is Machiavelli correct that the middle classes simply have the most power/votes and get the most benefits?*

If conventional government action cannot either redress moral wrongs or overcome social forces, how can it be considered moral? The stated reason for the U.S. government undertaking social welfare functions that were not enumerated in the Constitution was that private and local solutions were considered inadequate to meet the social catastrophe of the Great Depression. The local "protecting classes" in the 1930s could no longer convince the masses to limit national functions. Responsibility for general welfare was expanded again in the 1960s to meet the triple crises of poverty, senior ill health, and racial discrimination.[15] But these crises were not solved by the new programs either. Again, with an enormous expenditure of funds, the illegitimacy rate has continued to explode, most dramatically among black Americans. With great increases in government health spending and with enormous increases in health generally, the percentage of healthy birth weights among newborns has not improved either, with African-Americans again at the bottom.

Why do these programs not seem to work? One possibility is that, once initiated, these programs prove resistant to further reform. As Social Security and Medicare make clear, those already receiving benefits fear that changes to meet new situations will mean harm to their existing benefits. The result is the inability to take corrective action. To Nietzsche, this was the inevitable result of the misplaced pity of the weak, by Christians who had lost belief, with simple self-interest overriding any misplaced ideals of promoting the common good in the two largest programs of government. In fact, the World Bank data show that there has been a negative correlation between the amount the government spends as a percentage of national wealth and economic prosperity: the more government spending as a percent of national wealth, the less general welfare and prosperity. Moreover, without reform, these middle class programs are so large that, if they fail, the whole government could go down with them. As Aristotle noted, the proximate cause of the fall of nations usually is unwillingness to take the painful steps necessary to avoid bankruptcy—from Athens, to Rome, to Europe after World War I, to the Soviet Union, to Argentina today—even if the fundamental cause runs deeper.[16]

Might Islam have the last laugh again—that an inflexibility like the one that so fettered it during the rise of the West might now be seizing Europe and America? Or are the so-called solutions of the welfare state so obviously pale and ineffectual that even more basic changes in society are actually required, such as the fundamental ones demanded by Plato or Marx?

NOTES

1. Daniel Patrick Moynihan, "Defining Deviancy Down." *The American Scholar* (Winter 1993).

2. Charles Krauthammer, "Defining Deviancy Up," *The New Republic*, 22 November 1993.

3. Robert Putnam, *Bowling Alone* (New York: Simon & Schuster, 2000).

4. Andrew Carnegie, *The Gospel of Wealth* (London: F. D. Hagen, 1889).

5. Tocqueville, "What Sort of Despotism," in *Democracy in America*, II, 4, vi.

6. Schumpeter, "Crumbling Walls, *Capitalism, Socialism and Democracy*, chap. 12; Robert A. Nisbet, *The Quest for Community* (New York: Oxford University Press, 1953), chap. 5.

7. James Q. Wilson *The Moral Sense* (New York: The Free Press, 1993), 202.

8. Lewis Lehrman, "Capitalism: Only One Cheer," *Crisis* (April 2000).

9. George Ritzer, "The McDonaldization of Society," *Journal of American Culture*, vol. 6, no. 1, 1983.

10. See note 3 in chap 5, *supra*, and Donald Devine, *Restoring the Tenth Amendment* (Ft. Lauderdale: Vytis, 1996), chap. 4.

11. Gunnar Myrdal, *Beyond the Welfare State*, (New Haven, Conn.: Yale University Press, 1960) I, 5.

12. Frederic Bastiat, "How to Recognize Legal Plunder," in *The Law*, trans. Dean Russell (Irvington-on-Hudson, N.Y.: Foundation for Economic Education, 1950).

13. See Population Reference Bureau, at *www.prb.org* and *www.mrdowling.com* for this and all following population data cited in the text. Also see Tom Bethel, "Endangered Species," *The American Spectator* (September/October 2001), 61–67.

14. On the general problem of democracy and the particular example of Hitler see, Fareed Zakaria, *The Future of Freedom* (New York: Norton, 2003), 60 and 260 and chap. 5.

15. *Stastical Abstract of the United States* (Washington, D.C.: Government Printing Office, 1999); and "U.S. Preemie Rate Is Call to Action," *The Wall Street Journal*, 30 January 2003, D2.

16. Robert Skidelsky, *The Road from Serfdom* (New York: Allen Lane Penguin, 1995), 97.

Chapter Nine

Political Equality

WHAT IS EQUALITY?

Plato and Marx are emphatic that social problems can only be solved if something very fundamental is done to reconstitute existing society. To solve the problem of social decay, it is necessary to take drastic steps, not just tweak with conventional government planning. According to Marx, full equality in the ownership of property and the earning of income is necessary to produce social equality and happiness for all. Plato requires a society that would treat individuals, the sexes, and all other groups equally on the basis of each individual's moral merit. The Declaration of Independence also made equality—the premise that "all men are created equal"—the prerequisite for the good social order. Even modern supporters of limited government like Hayek make equally under the law the essential requirement. There is no way to avoid equality as an issue for the good society.

Before there was a single government for America, there were two peoples on the continent with very different ways of life that were forced into contact with each another. By international law, they were separate and equal nations and, in fact, originally negotiated formal treaties with each other. Even the U.S. Constitution—which was mostly silent about equality—gave the Congress the power to regulate commerce "with" the Indian tribes, using the same language as for foreign nations rather than for domestic states. In fact, the national government early assumed responsibility for the welfare of Native Americans, treating them as a client group. Soon, a third people appeared, but without protecting institutions like the tribe, there was not even the pretense to equality. Most African-Americans originally were brought to America as slaves. Slavery could have been prohibited by the Constitution, but the Southern colonies would not have entered the union on that basis, so it was tolerated nationally and legally enforced regionally. Likewise, women could have been given the right to vote by the Constitution, but qualifications for voting were mostly left to the states, which were not willing to grant this, at least at first. This general indifference to matters of equality, however, changed rather dramatically soon thereafter.

Equality For Native Americans?

Native Americans were the American continent's People Who Were Always Here. They were first and foremost a communal, tribal people who saw themselves as living in communion with nature. The migration of Europeans with their fundamentally different way of life was the critical factor in changing this reality and upsetting the established order for his native peoples, according to Chief Seattle.[1] Very soon, the communal People were simply inundated by individualist Europeans. Population mass changed everything, upsetting the whole balance of nature for the indigenous peoples. When there were too many Europeans, the native life-style could no longer be sustained. There were just too many to defeat in battle, even for a great warrior like Seattle, who became resigned and could only vaguely threaten the retribution of nature itself if whites abused their clearly superior powers. In an historic appeal from the heart, he was forced to tell his people they had no alternative but to obey the "good father" in Washington. While tribes remained the major means of organization, they became mere subjects of control by a national Bureau of Indian Affairs bureaucracy thereafter. Ever since, the welfare of Native Americans has been the clearest, longest, and most comprehensive welfare responsibility of the national government. Unfortunately, its record has been dismal in regard to this responsibility—with new fashions of toughness and compassion changing policy over time. At one point, President Andrew Jackson even refused to enforce a Supreme Court order to return Cherokee lands to their rightful owners.

Subsequent additional funding and more favorable attitudes toward the welfare of the native people still resulted in terrible poverty and widespread alcoholism on reservations right through to modern times. The government was even very recently declared in contempt of court for the manner in which it managed the tribes' private trust funds in a sympathetic, Democratic administration, under Bill Clinton, as well as into the following one of George W. Bush.[2] The funds are still tied up in court with no resolution. An extensive system of schools and health facilities was created, but neither worked, at least when compared to the European population, if that comparison is appropriate. Most every program was tried, but none resulted in greater equality or even much better welfare. For better or worse, individual freedom was generally subordinated to the tribe, apparently by the wishes of the native population. Even were the government willing, how could individual equality be imposed if Native Americans insisted on remaining in tribes?

Even if the vast government lands of the Western U.S. were restored to Native Americans as a matter of property right—would or should title be given to individuals or tribes? Various movements to return land to the natives have been proposed over time and some adopted. Other than the Alaska tribal corporations, most were not deemed especially successful. Recently, gambling has brought great wealth to many tribes and raised the question of whether more capitalism for tribes is the answer? Or should the present government management system continue? No one seems very optimistic about the viability of any of these solutions.

The Heroic Struggle for African-American Emancipation.

Unlike relations with the native peoples, the question of black slavery rested uneasily upon the American conscience from the beginning. Northern moderates like John Adams would have preferred to outlaw it entirely in the Constitution, but Southerners like Thomas Jefferson opposed it in theory but accepted it as a financial necessity. George Washington freed his slaves, but not until his death. Former slaves like Frederick Douglas were active in rousing the white populace to support its abolition. Some, like Harriet Tubman, were even more heroic, helping slaves escape the South through border Maryland to the North. While the following cataclysmic civil war eliminated slavery, it did not settle the problem of political equality for African-Americans. Indeed, the situation after slavery became more difficult in many ways. During Reconstruction, a rough political equality for African-Americans was enforced by union troops and life improved for many. When the troops were removed and voting rights were restored to the white majority, however, much of the resentment over the occupation was directed toward blacks. In the name of competitive presidential elections, majority rule meant non-enforcement by the national government of whatever potential lurked in the 14th Amendment, plus segregation laws in the South and social ostracism for blacks in the North. Majority rule and private discrimination turned out to be much more difficult to combat in a democracy than outright slavery.

A century after the elimination of slavery, Martin Luther King faced the fact that there was little prospect for equality for blacks in America without a new strategy. He, like Douglass before him, decided that shaming whites by appealing to their own values, was the best strategy and the superior moral course. He called equal treatment for African-Americans "a dream deeply rooted in the American dream" and argued that the Constitution and Declaration represented a "promissory note" for every American to achieve political equality. He recognized that he needed to rally the North against the greater evil of legal segregation, so his primary demand was for formal equality before the law, especially the elimination of "black code" segregation laws and barriers to the right to vote in the South. But he also had to challenge the more difficult "free discrimination" that was practiced up North.

Although King warned his fellow African-Americans against "the cup of bitterness and hatred," he did threaten also that "there will be neither rest nor tranquility in America until the Negro is granted his citizenship rights. The whirlwinds of revolt will continue to shake the foundations of our nation until the bright day of justice emerges." Undeniable injustices were listed in his appeal, as in the Declaration, such as police brutality, denial of lodging while traveling, and whites-only sections in transportation. It was moral disgust with these that led most Northern whites to demand reform, especially as reinforced in the media with dramatic pictures of police brutality restricting protestors in the South. Yet, King's appeal also pointed to future problems once legal equality was achieved, when he concluded: "We cannot be satisfied as long as a Negro in Mississippi cannot vote *and a Negro in New York believes he has nothing for which to vote.*"[3] Clearly, the later involved attitudes rather than the law, and that would prove much more difficult to address.

Legal Equality Before the Law Necessary and Sufficient?

To a great extent as a result of the moral forces unleashed by King and fortified by his and John Kennedy's assassinations, formal legal equality for African-Americans was achieved in law soon thereafter—through the passage of the Civil Rights Act of 1964, the public accommodations laws, and anti-employment discrimination regulations. Yet, simple legal equality before the law did not result in social equality. Concern about continued social discrimination that did not breach the new laws or unequal education or declining family situations or other racial problems created a demand for "affirmative action" by the government—to equalize matters for previously discriminated-against groups. Under Presidents Lyndon Johnson and Richard Nixon, preferences were granted in employment, education, and government contracting for racial minorities. For the first time since King, significant parts of the public and even the political leadership rejected the government solutions. Racial preferences, especially, turned many whites against at least parts of the civil rights program. Riots broke out, not in the South, but for the first time in the North. Referenda against "reverse discrimination" were passed by large margins even in liberal states, and courts ruled against any preference beyond equal protection. In spite of court orders, however, preferences were continued by government and regulated businesses both for fear of the political repercussions of their elimination and from a continuing concern for an African-American population that still was poorer than the majority and did less well in educational achievement. But continuing racial preferences did not result in social equality either.[4]

EQUALITY AND FREEDOM?

Precisely what would be required to achieve a society based upon equal justice for all? To Plato, current society must be "scraped clean" and a whole new social order created to achieve real equality and justice. The family would need to be abolished, together with private property, individual selection of a marital partner, exclusive sharing of a spouse, democracy, and more; or the presently advantaged families would continue to be wealthier and more successful than others. Marx makes similar demands, but the essential step for him is to divide property equally. All citizens must have the same income and wealth and equal amounts of the goods and services that can be purchased with them. The People want any program for justice or equality to be extended to all plants and animals too.

To what degree is equality desirable? Seattle and Eagle Man wondered whether full equality could survive in the face of migration from larger aggressive peoples that did not share these values. Aristotle valued virtue above equality, and even Plato placed justice higher. Locke ranked freedom as more important. De Tocqueville held that freely developed equality had many beneficial qualities for a society, but it also led to a certain lowering of standards and more acquiescence to authorities. Certainly, to him, equal incomes, communal sharing of children, and equality with plant life went much too far. There were other, competing values that also needed to be taken into account. In *The Federalist Papers*, while supporting moral equality, the Founders even argued that physical, intellectual, and wealth inequality are natural and cannot be suppressed without extinguishing freedom, which is like trying to eliminate air. So, is freedom more important than equality? Or is Marx correct that equality must first exist if there is to be real freedom later?

Which is More Important, Equality or Freedom?

1. *What did Jefferson mean when he wrote that "all men are created equal" when men were not equal anywhere in the world then or now? Equality*

was seen as unnatural to all societies before the Western ones—even to Aristotle. Plato had guardians above the people, not equality in the modern sense. All three accepted slavery, and it existed at the time he wrote, including in Jefferson's own Virginia. He owned slaves himself. What did he mean? What might Jefferson have meant if he only expected moral equality?

2. *Why are even obvious inequalities like slavery still ignored even today? If inequality is so bad, why is there so little interest in the issue of slavery in Sudan? A special ambassador—former Senator John Danforth— was appointed to pressure for its elimination, but not much happened. If the opposite of equality, slavery, is so wrong, why has no action at all been taken against Mauritania?*

3. *How about income inequality in the U.S. today? In the U.S., the top 5% of income earners receive 34% of total income and the bottom 50% earn only 13%. Most Western nations have about the same distribution. What is more, this degree of income inequality seems accepted in the West. Is this fair? The only problem is that third world nations have even more unequal income distributions.*

4. *In the U.S., the top 25% income earners (32 million people earning above $52,965 in adjusted gross income) in 1999 paid 83% of the income taxes and 75% (or 97 million) paid 17% of the taxes. The top 10% of income earners earned 45 percent of adjusted gross income and paid 67% of the income taxes. The bottom 50% earned 13% of income and paid 4% of the taxes.[5] 70 million citizens paid no income tax or got refundable tax credits. Is it fair to earn 66% of the income but pay 83% of the taxes? About 50 million Americans received government benefits of one type or another, including Social Security. Is it fair for the 30 million to support the 50 million? Can enough more be squeezed from the top to provide full equality even if that is what a majority desired? If all of the wealth of the top 1% were expropriated, it would run the government for only a few weeks. Moreover, the "top" is not necessarily very rich—the top 50% of income earners kicks in at as low as $26,415 per year.*

5. *Polls show that even low-earning Americans do not want all people to be paid the same because they do not want to foreclose the possibility they may become rich.[6] Obviously, many people would have to be re-educated in a very fundamental way to get them to support real equality. What does Plato mean when he said these values would need to be "scraped clean" for people to learn true values?*

6. *Students think the recommendation of Plato in the Republic are perverse because they think that Plato's ideal of equality can be picked and chosen from. Yet, Plato requires that children be separated from their parents*

and raised communally for a very important reason, because equality is impossible otherwise. One's mother and father give advantages (or disadvantages) to children. Do you not help your children? The only way to stop this is to never let parents know their children. It is the price in freedom to be paid to achieve true equality and justice.

7. *Plato's and Marx's programs are serious. They require fundamental changes in all areas of social life to achieve their ideals of equality. Women cannot raise children individually if they are to compete equally with men at work. The question is whether equality is worth the cost, or is freedom the higher value (not necessarily the highest)? Freedom clearly gives wealth—and opportunity too, at least to those with skills. Is this more important, or is equality?*

8. *While it is the people, presumably, who would benefit by equality, why is it that ordinary people seem to favor freedom more and intellectuals seem to prefer equality more? Why would freedom under fair rules seem more valuable than equality of results to poorer people as opposed to more well-off ones?*

9. *Market rationalization does bring radical change—some of it not predictable from the separate trades. But each separate trade is a free choice of people, unlike when government ignores popular opinion. Even democracies boast that representatives can ignore the popular will if it would lead to harmful legislation. Who can ask more of markets? Moreover, many of the negative results of trade, if not all, can be solved by charging people in the trade with the costs (even if unintended) of their actions by rational property incentives or in a rationalized tort system. But is this enough? Some people will still not use their freedom well.*

10. *What about all of the bad things that come directly from freedom? Would it not be better to get rid of freedom so the great evils that result from it do not occur? People are free to hurt as well as love. Certainly, Hitler, Stalin, and Mao are good reasons to limit freedom. They killed hundreds of millions of people. But that argument is with God or nature. Why did the Creator give this terrible freedom to human beings? Is that not a good reason to reject the very idea of Him? Might Hinduism be correct, that the world is irreversibly intractable, that there is no rational Creator that will make it all turn out right, and that all the best one can do is escape it through meditation and yoga?*

11. *Or can humanity do anything to stop this terrible freedom no matter what its view of the almighty? The Soviet Union certainly tried—but freedom broke through the cracks in the system anyway and brought this great power to destruction.*

STRATEGIES FOR EQUALITY TODAY

Among the forces that continue to inhibit equality, with freedom or without, is racism. Not surprisingly, strategies for dealing with it differ greatly. Many Americans, like author Richard Goldstein, see racism as powerful today as it was in the 1960s, requiring continued social ostracism and vigorous enforcement of the government programs enacted at the time and thereafter. Until there is full racial equality, affirmative action and even preferences for minorities will be required. Given the intractability of the problem, Goldstein demands additional criminal penalties for crimes committed against minorities beyond those required for the crime itself, "extra time for hate crime." But even that is not enough. Racist and homophobic "defamation" and "hate speech" among the majority is even more dangerous because it is protected by the First Amendment.

To combat this more insidious racism, Goldstein supports boycotts and demonstrations against those teaching "hate," giving the example of radio personality Dr. Laura. She apparently claimed that gay behavior was "deviant" and that gays used affirmative action laws to force straight society to accept their lifestyle. Noting that she was an Orthodox Jew, whose religion considers homosexuality sinful, Goldstein also observes she was only a "convert to Orthodox Judaism," suggesting that it was personal prejudice more than religious dogma. "She attacks like an old time anti-Semite," he argues. But this new bigotry reaches way beyond her to most "celebrity" radio "shock jocks" such as Don Imus. Their millions of listeners prove to him the widespread nature of bigotry these days. The cause of equality today "demands a constant assertion of values" and "righteous anger." Fascist thugs would not have gone so far 60 years ago in Germany if their hate speech were taken more seriously at the beginning, he concludes. Today, the celebrity bigots and their millions of racist fans need to be stopped "before it happens again" in the United States of America.[7]

Milton Friedman argues it is essential that a fundamental distinction be made between equality of opportunity and equality of results. Freedom is only consistent with the former, when government creates rules of law that allow all to compete equally under them for what people desire. Rules may be made fairer as long as no individual or group is given an advantage. But, as Madison and the rest noted, fair rules do not necessarily produce equal results. People have different talents and these lead to different outcomes and rewards. Is it fair that Muhammad Ali could make millions of dollars in one night in the boxing ring? Or is it unfair for government to deny, in the name of equality, this free choice by him and the fans willing to pay to see him fight? Government can never guarantee equal results without destroying freedom for at least some, if not all eventually, Friedman concludes. Private and true government charity, where taxes are assessed equally to pay for it, can make up the serious deficiencies, but requiring equal results will ultimately destroy risk, innovation, and reward and the prosperity that results from them.[8]

This logic applies equally to the area of race. If one race has a disproportionate number of people among the more successful, does this prove discrimination? Is it discrimination that most multi-millionaire professional boxers are African-American? Or do they just compete better under rules that reward natural skill? Why is it that "many people resent the inheritance of property but not the inheritance of talent?" There is no difference, Friedman says. Fairness under freedom means treating all equally under rules that apply equally to all. Fairness of results is often in the eye of the beholder and is impossible to establish in law without undermining equality under the law for others. When it advantages blacks to assure equality of results, government-administered affirmative action limits the freedom of some whites to compete, for example, in admission to college. What makes that fair? What is equal about demanding higher penalties for harming a person from one race as opposed to an equal injury to a person of another race? Is not hate in the heart difficult to apply as a general rule anyway? Is it applying an equality standard to consider one opinion on homosexuality—one that was, as Krauthammer noted, the official position of the psychological profession not that many years ago—as "hate," or is it fair to omit that the so-called "anti-Semite" Dr. Laura was born Jewish, although not orthodox?

What about those who are to be assisted by racial preferences? Author Shelby Steele is not so much interested in the negative consequences to the majority but to the minority. The biggest problem to him is that whites are helping blacks too much. Like de Tocqueville, he is concerned that if government does too much, it robs the individual of his freedom and right to compete. Guilt makes whites feel good when they pass laws granting preferences, but it robs blacks of their sense of humanness to achieve the "last test of true equality"—to become "fully competitive with others" under rules applied equally to all. This cannot be achieved if success is handed to people as a right by law. The historic Western solution of equality before the law is not only just, it is in the best interests even of those supposedly assisted by preferences. If laws advantage blacks, no one will ever think they earned anything on their own merit, and they will never win their rightful quest for true equality, concludes Steele.[9]

Malcolm X takes this a dramatic step further. He argues that African-Americans must solve all of their own problems and not rely upon whites at all. His solution is black nationalism, or the necessity for the "black man to control the politics and politicians in his own community." He is not afraid to call it "separation," which he claims is the only way to achieve black freedom in America. He relates that struggle to the one of Asians and Africans in throwing off the white man's colonialism in the 1960s. He threatened then to take the cause of blacks being bombed in their homes, little girls being murdered, and leaders assassinated in the U.S. to the United Nations or the World Court for solution. His call for using the "bullet" over the ballot is mostly for dramatic effect, but he takes pleasure in the image of a black man in the dark, with a knife, being "even-steven" with a more prosperous white. On the other hand, he says black dignity need not lead to bloodshed. All the country has to do is "give the black man in this country everything that's due him. Everything."[10]

EQUALITY OF RESULTS OR EQUALITY OF OPPORTUNITY?

How much and what kind of equality is necessary for the good society? What is wrong with a little affirmative action? Yes, it may limit equal opportunity based upon talent alone a bit, and "reverse discrimination" may disadvantage some. But is it not worth the small cost? It may violate Locke's and Hayek's prime requirement for a good political system that laws apply equally to all and not advantage special classes of citizens. But little of modern law does not advantage some group over another. Why does a bit more in the name of better racial equality make much difference? The United States has hardly become a tyranny after more than 30 years of affirmative action. How much does white guilt really hurt blacks? While social ostracism might mean stifled discussions on race for fear of being called racist or even conservative blacks being dismissed as "Uncle Tom's" (even if this includes the only black Supreme Court justice, the Secretary of State, and Steele), this could be justified on the grounds that it keeps many bigots from speaking hate. There is a reason that the political leadership has maintained affirmative action, even in the face of public opposition and Supreme Court rulings finding it undermining equality before the law. The reason is that opinion leaders and government officials believe that affirmative action is necessary and is the right thing to do morally. Would not anything else be cruel and insensitive to the plight of African-Americans?

But consider:

1. *Why did government "affirmative action" not work for Native Americans? Certainly there has been sufficient time to get results. In modern times, there even has been significant good will toward reform. Yet, even today,*

this government beneficence is a mess. In December 1999, Judge Royce Lamberth called the government's administration of the $500 million a year Trust Fund for Indians "fiscal and governmental irresponsibility in its purist form" and threatened judicial receivership. Earlier, in February, the Secretaries of the Interior and Treasury were cited for contempt for not producing court-ordered documents on the fund. The suit continues against the Bush Administration today. What could change the dynamics? How about returning all Interior federal land to Indians to manage as private, joint property, not necessarily in reparations but just to try something new? This would just substitute one public authority for another in an area the government went into reluctantly anyway (national parks began with a private grant from the Rockefellers) and does not manage well. Would not Native Americans—with their Peoples values—be more sensitive to the competing demands of the environment and the need for economic development? Would racism prevent this solution or would existing economic interests in the government and private welfare and environmental groups? If this were adopted, would it increase equality?

2. *Why does it take white evangelicals, rather than black Americans, to raise the issue of slavery in Sudan and Mauritania, the later of which has almost no Christians to be concerned about?*

3. *If affirmative action is so effective, why have three decades of its policies for African-Americans not worked? Is not permanent affirmative action an implicit admission that blacks are inferior?*

4. *Or has affirmative action simply not gone far enough? Is more enforcement necessary? Are even financial reparations required to achieve racial equality? Can such a tougher course earn the support of the majority or should it be enacted by authorities even without popular support?*

5. *Can compassionate majorities grant real power or do minorities have to seize it and create their own fair society, as Malcolm X suggested? Which states have the largest number of black elected officials, liberal New York or Massachusetts? No, Mississippi is first, Alabama second, and Louisiana third.*

6. *Can African-Americans peacefully solve the problem of equality all by themselves? The data demonstrate that all one has to do to become more equal financially is to get and stay married. A married black man in an intact family earns 80% of what whites do, compared to 55% for all blacks and whites (and it is probably 90% for long-term marriages). If blacks were married at the same rate as they were in the bad times of segregation, a statistical analysis suggests they would be virtually equal in income with whites.*

7. *Why was black illegitimacy so high in 2000 compared to 1950 when African-Americans were suffering far more greatly from segregation?*

8. *Steele's argument that government preferences are paternalistic attitudes that harm blacks and rob them of the satisfaction of competing and succeeding under fair rules is a strong one to the grandson of an Irish immigrant. The idea of earning dignity under rules that apply equally to all rings true. The author's Irish ancestors had as high an alcoholism rate as blacks do for drugs, and a high jail rate and broken families, too. In his humble opinion, if they had had modern levels of government support they would still be a poor and dependent minority.*

9. *Yet, there clearly seems to be something wrong. Is the equality of opportunity that results from competing under fair rules enough, or is something more required to produce social justice?*

NOTES

1. Chief Seattle, "Response to Governor Stevens," in *Indian Oratory* (Norman, Okla.: University of Oklahoma Press, 1971).

2. Paul Johnson, *A History of the American People* (New York: Harper-Collins, 1997), 490–523; "Indians Want Receiver for Trust Funds," *The Washington Post*, 22 October 2001, A17.

3. Martin Luther King, *I Have a Dream*, King Estate.

4. Johnson, *A History of the American People*, 887–97; Donald J. Devine, *The Political Culture of the United States* (Boston: Little Brown, 1972), 332–45; Donald J. Devine, *Does Freedom Work?* (Ottawa, Ill.: Caroline House, 1978), chap. 4.

5. *The Wall Street Journal*, 22 January 2002, p. A20.

6. Devine, *Political Culture*, 218.

7. Richard Goldstein, "Celebrity Bigots Why We Need Them and What They Won't Say," *The Village Voice*, 18 July 2000, 37–39.

8. Milton and Rose Friedman, "Equality of Opportunity," in *Free To Choose* (New York: Harcourt, 1979).

9. Shelby Steele, "Race and Responsibility," *The Wall Street Journal*, 18 January 1999, A18.

10. Malcolm X, "The Ballot or the Bullet," *Malcolm X Speaks* (New York: Pathfinder, 1989).

Chapter Ten

Social Justice

WHAT IS JUSTICE
AND WHAT DOES IT DEMAND, IF ANYTHING?

Even free marketer Adam Smith taught that no society could ignore the issue of justice. As important as was equality to Plato, justice was the preeminent virtue. But definitions of justice vary widely. Socrates' definition of justice as the virtue of being fair to all has been the most generally accepted one, even by those who did not support his version of what it meant to be fair. His foil, Glaucon, however, cynically defined "justice" as the mean between doing injustice to others—i.e., doing unfair things to people without getting caught, which is "good"—and having injustice (unfair things) done to oneself, which is bad. What we call justice is simply legalized power, which unnaturally restrains human nature's selfish essence only for the sake of civil order, without any moral content whatsoever. To Machiavelli, it was necessary only for successful rulers to *appear* just, and with a bit of wile the clever leader can fake fairness successfully as long as he does not take from them what they really care about, their property and their spouses. For actual justice, Plato's Republic noted that the property, spouses, and children people do care about were what led to selfishness rather than acting fairly, and that is why they had to be taken away and why the ruler had to be the most just rather than the most clever or most popular.

It should not be assumed that Plato's ideas are too impractical to be put into practice. In the sprawling and mighty Ottoman Empire, there was a kind of rule by a sultan philosopher king assisted by noble guardians. To a great extent selection was by merit, the fittest son survived to become sultan. His numerous brothers in the harem were legally killed at his accession, as the weak were to be in *The Republic*, to make succession conflicts, which drained Europe, less likely to threaten order. His bureaucracy was staffed with the brightest children of the sultan's Christian conquests (mostly from the Balkans), who were taken from their parents (who never saw them again) at an early age, forced to convert to the values of the society expressed by Islam, and educated in special schools how to administer the nation for the republic's (sultan's) benefit. Strangers and far from home, and whose children were not allowed to succeed to the highest offices that they filled nor the large properties they managed, the foreign Christians proved much more reliable guardians and less subversive than the native Turks. Indeed, most of the major Ottoman leaders below the sultan were forcibly converted Christian slaves. This Platonic republic was successful for five hundred years, lasting into the 20th century.[1]

Marx cannot simply be dismissed either. As with Plato, traditionalists most dislike his proposal to communize the family. But Marx argued that the cash calculation under capitalism had *already* destroyed the traditional family — only it did so brutally and unjustly and ended in inequality and decay. Capitalism's sharing of spouses took place through divorce and shunting away of children was to nannies and professional child centers. In fact, in the U.S., divorce did rise from 0.3 per 1,000 in 1860, when Marx wrote, to 3.5 in 1970 — more than ten times higher, and then up again to 4.7 in 1991, remaining roughly at that high level until today.[2] By modern times, the overwhelming majority of American mothers work outside of the home and leave their children to be cared for communally. Communism's promise to end the individualistic family simply does it with equality and fairness to all without the seaminess, selfishness, and decay of the same process under capitalism.

Consider Marx's ten-point program of 1848. It is about half adopted already in the West. He simply asks, why not go the rest of the way? Change need not be violent, either. Indeed, America will probably adopt communism without even realizing it. As noted, the capitalist Schumpeter recognized that the "mainspring" of the profit motive and the reason for work and saving under capitalism were to support a wife and several children. He predicted the traditional arrangements supporting capitalism would end when people's "inarticulate cost accounting" made them "aware of the heavy personal sacrifices that family ties, especially parenthood, entail under modern conditions."[3] In short, they would calculate that children cost too much, with college education and all, so they would have fewer of them. Is not the large bourgeois family already passé, dooming capitalism and guaranteeing the ultimate triumph of socialism and its regime of equality and justice for all?

But would the elimination of property actually promote equality? Even most progressives who are sympathetic to the equalization of property are not

sure on whether the costs would be too high. Parental advantage does guarantee some inequality, but eliminating the family goes too far and is unnec-
essary in any event. A more practical and less objectionable solution, as
Myrdal insisted, was for government experts to devise a permanent plan for
distributing incomes fairly, such as through progressive income taxes and
positive welfare programs for the poor. Even "alternative" single-parent and
childless "families" might even be able to reverse the course of their decay
with successful early intervention by expert school planners. Modern progressives like E. J. Dionne, however, have become sensitive to criticism that
the experts might abuse even this responsibility and talk about limits on their
power. Steven Weinberg—a modern liberal, frightened by the abuses of government power in the quest of perfect justice in the 20th century—goes so far
that he concludes that all utopias, including what he calls "the best and brightest" utopia of experts, have failed. He proposes what he calls a "half-utopia":
a civilized, egalitarian, and market-based society with only a few governmental programs to promote fairness—mostly just a progressive income tax.
Yet, he fears neither ordinary people nor political activists nor leaders will be
satisfied with this modest agenda. He worries that there is something in human nature, even after the horrors of the Holocaust, that requires a grandiose
communal experience to combat boredom, even to demand war—which he
deems "intolerable."[4]

Irving Kristol, a modern conservative, finds even this utopian—war is not
intolerable but still an option and even likely if history is any guide. Limits
on government power are still essential for evil will always exist; but why is
even a strong progressive income tax necessary or even fair? If the public
wants "basketball players" to make tens of millions of dollars, why is that unjust? A few "gloomy" economists like Ricardo and Malthus have hurt capitalism with their universal picture of ultimate doom and made socialism the
attractive alternative. But socialism does not work in a modern state. Capitalism does. It is, in fact, the only practical alternative. There should be equality
of opportunity and charity for those who cannot compete, but being fair to
everyone is impossible. Each person has his or her own definition of fairness.
The only solution is to provide fair rules under which people can live their
lives pretty much by their own individual efforts. The idea of social justice is
simply a socialist tool to break down the central Western idea of limited government—that there must and should be a large private sector where people
can be free to do what they want to achieve happiness without government
determining it for them. "Capitalism does not promise that much and does not
give you that much. All it gives is a greater abundance of material goods and
a great deal of freedom to cope with the problems of the human condition on
your own."[5]

But is even the minimalist "equal justice under law" possible today? Locke required that known rules be neutral and apply equally to all. As early as the 1960s, Hayek found that most American laws did not apply to all equally. There were special rules for all classes of people: farmers, union members, the elderly, urban residents, favored businesses, and many other groups received special treatment under the law. Tax rates were especially progressive and biased against the productive classes, not with an equal rate for all.[6] By the early 21st century, a serious legal analysis could argue that even basic legal protections were no longer applied equally. Ex-post facto laws were breached by ad hoc indictments against unpopular figures with new charges never written in statute or regulation beforehand, invented by prosecutors after the fact. Self-incrimination protections were overridden by zealous prosecutors harassing defendants into plea bargains —which by the 21st century represented 90 percent of criminal convictions in the U.S.—in a kind of modern torture through media leaks and defamation.[7] Only 10 percent of criminal justice claims are settled through juries and courts. What is left of a system that justifies itself on equality before the law that does not provide it? Or, in a time with widespread threats of terrorism, more sophisticated criminals using more advanced technology, and more tenacious social pathologies, must the old procedural rights be modified to keep peace and order?

So, what is necessary for justice—must society guarantee fairness to all or be deemed a failure? Must fairness include full equality? Or is equality of opportunity—i.e., fair rules—and fair enforcement enough? Or is even equality before the law less important than social order and the guarantee of sufficient welfare for all?

1. *Is complete and universal fairness possible? Is it fair that some men (or women) get the attractive spouses just because they were born handsome? Why, following Plato, should not spouses be shared by all? Would that not be the only fair way?*

2. *Was Marx right, are we already sharing spouses? Is that right or wrong, or does it not matter?*

3. *Justice will obviously require sacrifice—why is a communal child-rearing system not a low enough cost for such an enormous gain?*

4. *Can great ideals such as those of Plato and Marx be implemented successfully? Or is Smith right that justice needs to have a narrow definition or the government is given a job no one can handle fairly? When the government tries to do it, does it create more problems than it solves?*

5. *Does the fairness definition of justice just transfer the problem of unfairness from individuals acting unfairly to the government acting unfairly?*

6. *Is justice possible without seriously limiting freedom if it is defined so expansively as to require fairness in everything and everyone? Do not all*

of the arguments in favor of freedom verses equality likewise apply to justice? Which is more important, freedom or justice?

7. *Does one have to choose between freedom and justice? The philosopher Edmund Burke said that the solution was easy: freedom is essential to justice, so that justice cannot be defined so broadly as to exclude freedom.*

8. *But defining justice as fair rules is difficult even in the United States, to say nothing about less successful free nations, so is that even a solution?*

9. *Only one modern form of government tries to guarantee ideal justice to all, in every way, Islam. Is Shari'a the answer?*

10. *Or is Plato not correct once again? With all of the evil in the world in all of the existing societies, must we not morally accept what needs to be done and create the ideal republic that places justice as the single, highest goal for society, no matter what the costs?*

FEMALE JUSTICE:
LEGAL EQUALITY, SOCIAL EQUALITY, OR FAMILY?

While perhaps not reaching the Platonic ideal, Elizabeth Cady Stanton's "Declaration" is about as bold a call for female equality and justice as ever developed. With a confidence rivaling its earlier Declaration model, she documents her complaints of unfair treatment of women: (1) by the government, in denying the vote, representation, and political rights; (2) in the family, in vesting property rights and even some criminal liabilities exclusively in the husband, restricting grounds for female divorce, and making women responsible for rearing children; (3) in work and education, requiring a single woman to pay high taxes but having the best occupations closed to her; and (4) regarding morals, not admitting women to prestigious roles like the ministry but granting to men the power to "destroy her confidence" in her social worth. To say the least, this is an interesting and comprehensive mix of concerns.[8]

The complaints against denial of governmental rights are conventional and were probably well accepted by most in her audience even then. The concerns about the family, however, were more controversial. Some, perhaps many, women may have liked the idea that male property ownership brought with it his culpability for its misuse, including that imprisonment for debt on their property could be borne by the husband even if the wife was at fault. The idea that he was responsible for certain crimes might have had appeal too. And, when men rather than the government were able to punish their wives for certain crimes, might not a husband chastise his wife more softly than the state?

The work complaints went in the opposite direction. If single women were to be equal, should they not pay as high taxes as men? Single women were in many occupations, but not many of them were in "male" occupations. Was this men's fault or was it women's unwillingness to start businesses themselves to enter these occupations—because, in most cases, the bar was not legal but social? The idea of men destroying women's confidence was especially strange for someone preaching female power and equality—could anyone have destroyed Stanton's confidence? For the others, do women have a moral or legal right to have their confidence boosted? How about men?

These "problems" are easily explained by the fact that the "Declaration" was a political document. It sought to build a coalition in favor of justice, broadly defined, for women. Much of her support was from single women, which explains the "high taxes" concern. Her proposals to eliminate preferences for married women probably account for the weak support she received at the 1848 Woman's Convention. Her Declaration was signed by only one-third of these potentially friendly delegates and some who signed recanted later. By the time Stanton wrote her autobiography fifty years later she was concerned she still had not convinced many women even to demand the vote for themselves.[9] Her emphasis upon temperance legislation and liberal divorce laws probably cost some more support as well as won some. As some of her modern supporters assert, the weak support may have been the result of male pressure but, maybe, the women of that day were not as helpless this picture implies. When women's attitudes clearly changed in the early 1900s, both temperance and the right to vote passed the tremendous barrier of Constitutional amendments within a year of one another—before women even had gained political power through the right to vote!

Stanton already saw in 1898 that social beliefs such as how a woman should be "properly" dressed—bloomers were considered "immodest"—that roles in private and church governance, and even that interpretation of the Bible and moral matters would be more important for full equality than political rights. Long before laws were changed, Stanton, herself, contracted an equal—striking "obey" from her marriage contract—and satisfying marriage and was a great supporter of the institution. But many feminists of the day viewed marriage itself as the problem. The writer Kate Chopin even had marriage literally kill her heroine, Louise, in her most famous short story.[10] It may have taken a long time for Stanton to get things started, but once attitudes were changed, they moved quickly. By World War II, the popular intellectual Virginia Woolf could argue that the moment of full legal equality had finally arrived for women. But social equality had not. "Phantoms and obstacles" were "looming in the way" of true equality, especially the myth of the "angel in the house," which made the unselfish mother the ideal for womanhood. A bit of selfishness is not all a bad thing for the female character, Woolf re-torted. It is not men but women themselves who must overcome these phan-toms—including the myth of family duty—if they ever were to be really free.[11]

By the 1990s, Naomi Wolf could argue that the "masculine empire" was "dying." Indeed, she warned that the only threat now is from females them-selves, if women become too nasty to men in the process of taking power from them and provoke a reaction. Female assertiveness has won the day, and victory only required a bit of common sense on the part of women. Marriage no longer binds women more than men. In fact, women—being a majority of college graduates—are becoming dominant in politics, culture, and the criti-cal professions such as law.[12] The modern critical feminist Christina Hoff Sommers goes to the point of claiming that men, boys, had now become the oppressed sex. Boys are a year and a half behind girls in reading and writing in school and are less likely to go to college and are behind socially in many ways. She blames traditional feminist flawed research—she mentions Har-vard's Gender Professor, Carol Gilligan—and women activists for the reverse perception of girls being weaker in school and the attack on boys that it in-spired. These did just what Wolf feared and pressed their gains too far. To win their point, these modern feminists even brought back the myth of superior women "nurturers and caretakers"—reviving the image Woolf so abhorred—now making it apply to both boys and girls. In this, Sommers argues, they are "deeply disrespectful" of boys—to insist on raising them like girls, seriously damaging their social development in the process.[13]

There even is a "new feminism" that is more sympathetic to the tradi-tional role of motherhood and is less sure that selfishness is a positive de-velopment. Danielle Crittenden argues that the problem goes beyond boys. Every woman knows what her child—boy or girl—needs most is her. Yet, in the modern era, she wants the rewards of work too—contributing to a form of "madness" in trying to do everything. Most women would prefer, in an ideal world, to stay home with their young children. In fact, they think of their children all of the time and feel guilty for not being with and helping them. But by this time, the selfishness Woolf advocated has per-manently become a partially defining aspect of female culture and so mothers still also crave the rewards of work. Modern woman remains torn between the needs of her children and her desire for rewarding work, free-dom, and independent income. She ends asking, have women "simply traded one form of unhappiness for another?"[14]

What about the children? Whatever the attitude of women, it is clear that children receive less attention from them—and men—on the average of about ten hours less per week from 1960 to 1986, according to one study. As for the men, Marx found a century and a half ago that Western men take their "greatest pleasure in seducing each other's wives," not caring for their children. Another study found the amount of time that the average child spent interacting with a parent declined 43 percent, from 30 hours a week to about 17 hours today. One-fifth of children aged 5 to 14 were latchkey children who took care of themselves outside of school hours during the day.[15] With no parent at home, children are placed in day care every day for many hours—government schools forcibly keep children attending classes all day (stay-in-school laws)—and are left on their own otherwise. While women's rights relative to men's are surely higher than in the 19th century, children are probably emotionally worse off, especially without intact families. Child abuse is 33 times more likely in single-parent homes, and a 1996 Health and Human Services study found that child abuse is most likely from a single mother, next most likely from a live-in cohabiting boyfriend, and least likely when a married father and mother are present in the home.[16]

But what is so special about children? If women are left responsible for children, they cannot compete equally with men in the marketplace. Are not her needs and desires more important? One option is to remain single. As Crittenden notes, single women make 98 percent as much as men, essentially the same. But, as she also notes, women want to be married and have children. Why should she be denied either motherhood or equality of earnings? Why can she not have motherhood and rewarding business leadership?

How else could she obtain full sexual equality and career social justice?

1. *Is Madonna not the perfect role model for the modern career woman, the material girl shorn of all traditional family values? Woolf would appreciate her assertiveness. She totally rejected the "angel" role during her youth, refused marriage for childbirth, became a multi-millionaire businesswoman, and was adored by millions. When her youth was fading, she hooked up with a rich man and now brags that she has never changed a diaper. Recently she tried marriage. Why not teach your daughter to emulate her success? After all, she could be rich and famous too.*

2. *The poverty rate for married, two-parent families is 4.7% living in poverty compared to 42% in poverty for female-headed single-parent families. Is the "powerful single life" a life-style that should be promoted to most young women?*

3. *The Marine Corps refuses to treat women equally in military training or in the infantry, even under incredible political pressure, citing the lower standards in the Army where this did take place. Special forces in all of the military services, like those active in Afghanistan and Iraq, refuse women in their ranks. Is this unfair, unjust?*

4. *The recent terrorism attacks revealed that of more than 11,000 fire peo-ple in New York City, only 68 were women. Are civil rights laws being vi-olated? Does this violate justice?*

5. *Government figures show that men represent 93.3% of the nation's two million prisoners and women only 6.7%. Is this discrimination?*

6. *How can it be just that in the 21st century women still earn only 57% of what men do? Are women still forcefully segregated in traditional women's occupations by male social pressure? Or are the gaps simply the result of female choices of desired occupations or choices concerning flexible time schedules for different work or childrearing interests?*

7. *Single women who have never had children earn essentially the same as men. Is the 57% difference in pay between women and men generally the result of discrimination or the unwillingness of women to deny them-selves motherhood?*

8. *Is the injustice an inequality of income or that children are not being cared for? Is it just me over my child, as Crittenden asks?*

9. *Do children really need special care and protection by mothers? The postmodernists Baber and Murray want completely open sex roles with no sex especially responsible for children. They only shrink from adult-child sexual relationships. But why that qualification? The Man-Boy Love Association thinks adult sex with a child is fine. If there are no moral limits for sex roles, why should there be any special moral limits for age roles? Since their hearts tell them it is good, why should they not be able to make love with children? How can love be wrong or unjust?*

10. *Or is the injustice truly the fault of men? The anthropologist Margaret Mead argued that the major problems of society may be clearly per-ceived in pictures of primitive peoples. Young women and old men are smiling; young men and old women look angry and resentful. Both of the angry groups are male problems today: men do not stay to raise boys or care for older wives. Are men tough enough to stay at home even in the face of cellulites, as Gloria Steinham put it? Or is it just me over my family?*

11. *What happens when it is all me? Europe had a 1.7 childbearing rate (al-ready 20% below replacement) as recently as 1990 but has a mere 1.4 rate today For many years, the U.S. has been just below the replacement rate of 2.1 births per child-baring age woman. As early as 2050, Italy (with a "replacement" rate of merely 1.2%!) or Spain will be depopu-lated or could have Muslim majorities. On the other hand, Muslim coun-tries have high child replacement rates: Somalia has a child replacement rate of 7.1%, Saudi Arabia has 6.3%, Iraq 4.9%, Pakistan 4.6%, and In-donesia 2.6%. Which civilization will be successful in the long run?*

12. *A solution to the decline in childbearing in the West favored by Crittenden is a "family policy" to pay families to encourage having children. In the U.S, this will be very difficult since so much of future resources are pledged to go to the elderly (e.g., Social Security, Medicare, much of Medicaid, and government pensions). Question: which is fairer, giving priority to children or the elderly? Even with great resources devoted to family policy—Sweden has dedicated 5% of GDP since 1990 to family policy, and France and Germany have devoted vast sums too—population still keeps going down*
13. *Population does count, as Eagle Man and Seattle insisted. Without children and subsequently enough adults, nations die.*

Islam has a simple answer: God says that it is the woman's duty to have children and the man's to support her and any naturally resulting offspring. Then nations grow. The same God commanded the West to do likewise, but it turned its back on Him and pursued selfishness instead. Worse, through Hollywood and television, it has spewed its pagan immorality to the whole world so that no one can escape it. Rather than promote the family, it promotes cohabitation, same-sex marriage, and faithlessness in marriage. Every successful civilization has encouraged the traditional family and knows what is essential to make it work. God's justice simply requires that all do their duty. Women must stay home enough to care for the children, and men must stay and work for them. Only Islam offers the law of Shari'a to enforce the obviously proper way to act, based upon one man and one woman in a faithful marriage. Since only Muslims today procreate and the West is not replacing itself, Islam must have the last laugh and overcome and even re-populate the West. Italy and Spain are won already and could be majority Islam by the middle of the century. Westerners simply have lost the moral will to reproduce themselves. As its numbers prove, ultimately the U.S. will follow, too, only at a slower rate. In a century, Islam will have triumphed.

Unless Islam changes substantially, the results would be:

1. *Freedom would not be as high a priority. The law would rule. The Freedom House study shows that only one Muslim nation rates as "free," Mali, and that is in the lowest free category of a 2.5 rating; 18 are partially free (39%) and 28 are unfree (59%). Only 23% of these countries even have a nominal outward form of democracy by holding elections.*[17]
2. *Females would be treated very differently than in the West, and certainly not more equally. Women's roles would clearly be closely confined to the family*
3. *There would probably be more international conflict. Muslims represented 20% of the world's population but 26 of the 50—or a majority of the*

national or ethnic conflicts in the world in the 1990s.[18] *But that is how a triumphal civilization assures its dominance.*

So what? Every American alive today would be dead by then. In the meantime, women would have equality, freedom, and self-fulfillment for themselves, and men could escape the rugrats, the cellulites, and the work — and have fun too. What is wrong with that?

NOTES

1. Lord Kinross, *The Ottoman Centuries* (New York: Harper-Collins, 2000), 33–36 and 146–153. The author makes a direct comparison to Plato's Republic on p. 150. Marx might be pleased that, with no hereditary or private property, there was equal opportunity among the Christian slaves, whose promotions were then strictly based upon merit (153), except for the sultan, who also had to be adroit in order to rule over his brothers to assure he escaped the legal death sentence awaiting the losers.

2. *Historical Statistics of the United States* (Washington, D.C.: Bureau of the Census, 1971), I, B.

3. Joseph A. Schumpeter, *Capitalism, Socialism and Democracy* (New York: Harper and Row, 1950), 157.

4. Steven Weinberg, "Five and a Half Utopias," *The Atlantic Monthly*, January 2000.

5. Irving Kristol, "A Capitalist Conception of Justice," in Richard T. DeGeorge and Joseph Pilcher, eds., *Ethics, Free Enterprise and Public Policy* (New York: Oxford University Press, 1978).

6. Hayek, *Constitution of Liberty*, 228–33 and 244–49 and Chs. 17–24.

7. Paul Craig Roberts and Lawrence M. Stratton, *The Tyranny of Good Intentions* (Rosedale, Calif.: Prima, 2000).Also see John S. Baker, Jr., "An Injustice in Houston," *The Wall Street Journal*, 18 June 2002, A16.

8. Elizabeth Cady Stanton, *Declaration of Sentiments* (New York: R. J. Johnson, 1870).

9. Elizabeth Cady Stanton, *Eighty Years and More* (New York: European Publishing Co., 1897).

10. Kate Chopin, "The Story of an Hour," in *The Awakening and Other Stories* (Chicago: H. S. Stone & Co., 1898).

11. Virginia Woolf, "Professions for Women," in *Death of the Moth and Other Essays* (New York: Harcourt, 1942).

12. Naomi Wolfe, "The Decline of the Masculine Empire," in *Fire With Fire* (New York: Random House, 1993), 17–24.

13. Christine Hoff Sommers, "The War Against Boys," *The Atlantic Monthly* (May 2000), 59–74.

14. Danielle Crittenden, "The Mother of All Problems," *Saturday Night* (April 1996), 44 ff.

15. James Q. Wilson, *The Moral Sense* (New York: The Free Press, 1993), 159, and George F. Will, "Lethal Reticence," *The Washington Post*, 7 June 2001, A26.

16. *The Kids Are Alright? Well Being and the Rise of Cohabitation* (Washington, D.C.: The Urban Institute, July 2002).

17. "New Study Details Islamic World's Democracy Deficit," *Freedom House*, 18 December 2001, <http://www.freeedomhouse.org>.

18. Samuel P. Huntington, *The Clash of Civilizations and the Remaking of the World Order*, (New York: Simon & Schuster, 1996), 254–65.

Chapter Eleven

Business and Work Responsibility

HAVING FUN YET?

Marx is the philosopher of fun. His fun is opposed to the "serious happiness" taught by Aristotle and passed through the Western tradition into the Declaration, one that required duty and even sacrifice of one's life and fortune. Once the leadership class produced by this unfun capitalism is disposed of, Marx says that human beings will then be free to enjoy nature with poetry in the morning, meaningful work during the day if one wants, or enjoyable play, good food and drink, and sex and fun at night. No problem! The American, Thoreau, likewise sees nature as the source of pleasure and capitalist rules and restrictions as what make life unpleasant. He argues that man must be free of tradition and its restraints to truly enjoy life. Man is to pursue his own pleasure not that of the community or of some organized moral system. Thoreau's escape to nature in Walden Pond freed him from the demands of organized society and government. On the other hand, Thoreau's is a more "serious" fun than Marx's, requiring some co-existence with nature. Although they would blanch at the idea, both Marx and Thoreau desire something like a laissez faire market free from Western rules on property, law, and morals. That would be perfect freedom, and it would be fun.

So far, efforts to end conflict and the rules to contain it so that human beings can live the life of fun have not proved successful. Instead, pro-market theorist Adam Smith argued that the government could produce sufficient happiness if it just limited its role to protecting individuals from injury and relied upon the free harmony of private interests, or the "invisible hand," in a market to create enough wealth and welfare for all to live reasonably well. But progressive theorists like Myrdal found that this free harmony assumption was proved wrong by the "market failure" of the Great Depression, and it was abandoned. In its place, experts planned commerce rationally to eliminate gloomy economic outcomes and bad times, with planned regulatory and welfare programs that would provide fun for all. If the Federal Reserve controlled market downturns and Health and Human Services provided life support for millions who would otherwise be denied it, this new welfare state would result in practical fun for everyone.

Modern market theorists like Schumpeter and Hayek argued that, in fact, history proved that the welfare state ultimately fetters the creation of wealth in the market as it goes beyond setting general rules, because the experts have no way to know how to control the vast complexity of the billions of market transactions that take place every day in it. There is also a type of "government failure" that leads to plunder that subverts goals and programs and leads to inefficiency and, ultimately, to bankruptcy. The Soviet Union had great experts but with no price mechanism, they could not tell what or how much or when or where to produce or to distribute goods and services. If you distort those price mechanisms by government fiat, this disrupts communication and leads to breakdown, as it did in the Depression, which can be argued was a government failure rather than a private one—and was not fun.

The Nobel laureate Milton Friedman and his associates were the ones who provided the unpleasant news that the Federal Reserve might have provoked the 1930s depression by not expanding the money supply quickly enough. Another theory was that the President, following the advice of economic experts, provoked it by jawboning wages flat. In either case, it was the government that failed and created unhappiness, not the market, they argued.[1] These economists argue aggressively that the profit mechanism is the way the market signals supply and demand to make it work. Profit provides the incentive to grow and prosper as it signals to capitalists what people will pay for and thus leads them to success and prosperity. Profit cannot only be distributed or invested for additional productivity to produce greater wealth, but it also supports the taxes for a more effective government to keep the internal peace and to protect against foreign threats—for peace, too, is generally a precondition for good business. While government can disrupt these signals—as the Federal Reserve Bank did in 1929 with terrible consequences—so can business itself. Managers do so if they do not use profit to guide their decision-making. If they do not follow the price signals, markets cannot work efficiently and will fail. Even if they try to do good rather than obey the profit signals, they will direct resources inefficiently and will not give the owners their due.[2]

Thus, not following the market might also reduce the fun for many. Friedman argues that top managers are simply well-paid employees and are required to serve the interest of the owners, the stockholders in a modern capitalist system, who have the moral claim to the rewards. This is especially important today when workers' pensions own the majority of stock. In the 2002 Enron scandal, it was the pension system that suffered the major loss from the decline in stock prices. Is it possible that pursuing callus profit is the moral course? Critic Christopher Stone argues that Friedman is wrong, presenting various legal limitations the government has already set as social welfare goals for the market other than profit. Has this not ruined the market but resulted in a more rationally planned economic and welfare system? Still, even he concedes that managers could go too far following their own "vague and various notions of what is good for the rest of us" and that the market through its stockholders and financiers does rightly limit how far management can go in promoting charitable fun over profits.[3]

Marx counters that the only problem is that Stone's welfare state does not go far enough so that government failure is truly eliminated so that all can be happy. It can only do this when private property is abolished and the state is ended and withers away so that people can at last concentrate on having fun. It is the staid Declaration and its progeny that resist this modern search for fun. The Declaration says that happiness derives from inalienable rights granted by a Creator to individuals. Because they come from a higher source, government cannot properly take away these rights—as the British did to provoke the American Revolution—even if government's stated goal is to produce more fun. Moreover, even that revolution had to be justified to this "Supreme Judge." The problem is He demands work and even sacrifice to earn His brand of happiness. Individuals may pursue happiness only where the law does not forbid it, Locke taught, either Divine or human law. The Declaration even pledges the signers' lives and "sacred honor" to the cause—not much fun if you lose, which was very likely when one was trying to break away from the most powerful empire in the world. Happiness results from difficult, committed work like that which was required to create the new nation, not from fun, these spoilsports say. Or does anyone care what these old, white, European males say is necessary to achieve human happiness?

PURSUIT OF HAPPINESS OR PURSUIT OF FUN?

So is it Pursuit of Happiness or Pursuit of Fun, or Neither?

1. *As the World Bank and Freedom House data make clear, the free market clearly produces enough wealth for fun in the West, especially in the U.S. But there is also great dissatisfaction there, just as Schumpeter predicted. If we are so free and rich, "Why aren't we having fun yet?"*

2. *Do we need to try harder? Can the new morality of health and fitness replace the old stoic virtues and finally produce fun? Can technological inventions like bio-engineering or cloning finally deliver endless good health and fun? Can even death be eliminated? Can fun be forever?*

3. *With fun unlikely from the market, can government step in to produce more fun? Yet, as everyone from Socrates and Aristotle on down predicted—democratic government cannot say "no" and plunder, inefficiency, and insolvency (e.g., Social Security) are the result. Might democracy like the market and the fun and freedom they produce only be temporary until the bills come due?*

4. *Why cannot business solve its own problems of work and production? The problem, Schumpeter noted, is that "The stock exchange is a poor substitute for the Holy Grail," as the "genius in the business office may be and often is utterly unable outside of it to say boo to a goose." Businessmen cannot defend their values or institutions against clever anti-market intellectuals in the media or bureaucracy or resourceful political leaders because they are practical rather than cultural, theoretical, or mystical. Businessmen have no prestige to match the Holy Grail nor the Constitution nor a good philosopher nor even a sharp politician. They only have money and that only buys intellectual support as long as it is paid, money that can easily be taken away by government power. So, the pull of politics and culture weakens capitalist interests as tycoon victims from Michael Milken to Charles Keating to Clark Clifford to Robert Altman to Bill Gates could testify.*

5. *Can more modern and prudent liberal intellectuals like Walzer, Dionne, and Weinberg provide the necessary commitment? They recognize the need for more market rationality and the need to limit political demands so that government's reach does not subsume freedom and destroy market efficiency. But where does one draw the line? They have few suggestions. Without one, markets become increasingly fettered and more progressive programs produce more perverse results or go bankrupt or both.*

6. *But the parties of the right cannot resist the trend either. George W. Bush set a 4% budget increase as the maximum allowable for sound economic growth when he first became president. But even before 9/11/01, he had agreed to 6%, a one-third increase, and about the Bill Clinton average. Subsequently he accepted an 8% increase, double what he had said was safe to spend. In a democracy, can no one say no to "more" fun?*

7. *So is Schumpeter correct: The market system with all of its great freedom and prosperity cannot survive because it has no one to protect it from its excesses?*

8. *Schumpeter, Adams, and Jefferson all argued that only an aristocracy—real in England, natural and agricultural in the U.S.—ever allowed the market to work in a democracy because it had independent and local power that allowed it to protect other people's property from demagogues as they protected their own. This elite's "prestige was so great and [its] attitude so useful that the class prestige long outlived" its riches and power, for England "right to the end of the period of intact and vital capitalism." Without their noble, feudal occupations, powers, and values—of the warrior, the lord with his "halo," the priest, the local community leader or squire, and the craft guild master-worker—there was no one to protect the bourgeois from demagogues who provoked the masses to attack property so they could have the funds to produce ever more fun. Once the prestige and property of the old leadership were gone, often due to the bourgeois themselves taxing and regulating it, there was no one to close the floodgates. It certainly would be strange if an aristocracy were necessary to preserve democracy, but life is full of paradoxes; yet, it probably would be impossible to recreate one anywhere in the West anyway.*

9. *Can the military keep a market and democratic society going? But the military is the prime example of the old code of duty, honor, and sacrifice for country—the question is can the military coexist with a society based upon fun? It is not fun to kill or be killed. So, heh, the military is, like, a drag. Until 9/11, the warrior class was even called murderers and pigs by many blooming intellectuals and their training (outside the Marines and elite Army/Navy/Air Force special operations units) was made more like that of the Girl Scouts than 1950s basic training. Spying, especially, was considered a drag. Fun people (a former defense secretary said "gentlemen") do not read each other's mail, nor lie, nor get shot in exotic locales, nor is any of this remotely fun. Sensing cultural distain for warriors and spies, bin Laden smelled weakness and struck hard.*

10. *Is it just fine for society if all of the men follow Thoreau and go to the forest to have fun? Why not? Who will charge the machine guns and go cut the throats on the suicide missions? Demi Moore? Can the U.S. survive the loss of the traditional civic values that have made its military ethos so successful and sustain its recruitment—which is still primarily rural to this very day? Or might the majority recover the noble virtues and eliminate the values gulf? Or should they? Why should not each person just grasp for fun?*

11. *If sacrifice matters, does the revival of the prestige of the protecting occupations since 9/11 imply there is some chance of renewal? Or was it momentary? The end of October 2001 enlistment figures showed, in con-*

trast to earlier predictions based upon the greater patriotism evident from the wide display of flags after 9/11, no increase in military enlistments. Is flag-waving enough or is actual sacrifice required?

12. *Or doesn't sacrifice matter? The French army did not know about its loss of noble virtue until it took up positions in 1940 and fell apart. Fun did not work against Hitler. But life went on, Hitler passed, and the time for play has appeared again, has it not?*

WORK OR PLAY?

Play is the fun alternative to work. The British poet W. H. Auden called non-fun work, "labor." The favored classes—the aristocrats—have always tried to avoid labor, live off the masses' sweat, and play. Both he and Nobel Laureate Bertrand Russell believed that fulfilling work was available only to a fortunate few, at least until all are freed in a true Marxist utopia. Auden gave precise figures: 84 percent of people labor, and only 16 percent work but view their work as play. The problem was the vast majority is subject to boredom, and the history of how the aristocracy played is not reassuring for what ordinary people with boring jobs will do—drunkenness [drugs], whoring, destroying family, undermining heroic values—these would seem the future for all in a mass democracy, not just the rich.[4] Russell is more optimistic in the sense that "even the dullest work is to most people less painful than idleness," so ordinary people are not totally without fun. Yet, this is really not fun but only "less painful" than doing nothing. He is even fatalistic about the highest-level work, that which can be considered play. He says that he cannot "maintain that even the greatest work must make a man happy; we can only maintain it will make him less unhappy." The vast majority, however, cannot attain even being less unhappy.[5] The existential writer Albert Camus is even more of a drag. He fatalistically looks at all life as an unavoidable lifting of rocks. Work is what humans do, and the only satisfaction is to knowingly "negate the gods," to know life is meaningless other than the lifting.

Progressives remain optimistic that democratic participation can provide meaning, including for work. Labor analyst David Ewing believes that government can establish democratic rights against employers so that ordinary workers can be happy in their jobs. People need jobs to survive, but unionization can make working conditions pleasant and work meaningful. Unions are the democratic solution to make the employee equal to the employer in power, backed up with legal rights won for them with this power.[6] As Marx predicted, workers obtain rights through union-oriented political parties. Unions can also act through confrontation and even violence. Strikers cannot be arrested in West Virginia, and police (also in unions) often turn their back on union violence (e.g., the *New York Daily News* strike). It is clear that this is real power—at least when the union party is in charge—but does it produce meaningful work? The adversarial situation created with management and within government may even increase dissatisfaction, and even these hard-won economic gains in single nations are now threatened by global competition.

The basic idea of a union is solidarity—to work-to-a-rule so that no one will work beyond the rule and thus be unfair to his weaker, less capable fellow workers. The majority rules in a union, and only a minority, as Auden noted, work hard or creatively. Perhaps 20 percent of workers do 60 percent of the work in many situations. The union ideal is to divide the work equally and discipline or fire no one. Government unions—the only growing union sector—have basically achieved this goal. Private labor unions cannot compete in world markets with these restrictive rules that encourage play over labor, and so they are in serious decline. Consequently, the political power of unions is the main reason that world free trade has not advanced further in the U.S. Congress, to the great disadvantage of the third world—a case made most effectively by Thomas Friedman, a liberal *New York Times* columnist, in his incredibly successful book, *The Lexus and the Olive Tree*.[7] In spite of union efforts, most of the countries of the world agreed in early 2002 to further loosen trade barriers to allow workers worldwide to compete under rules of work rather than union dreams of fun. But dreams are what people are made of and why Marx and Plato will never die and why the new trade round may still never see the light of day.

PUSHING ROCKS?

Even most businessmen prefer fun to laborious work or tough-minded competition. Political science studies show that, whatever their abstract commitment to the market, businessmen often are the source of demands for market regulation to protect their own existing market share.[8] Even when forced to compete in the market, businessmen often try to escape its discipline. A famous play by Jerry Sterner, *Other Peoples' Money,* which also became a motion picture, features the businessman Andrew Jorgenson who is struggling to preserve his 73-year-old family firm. It is a mainstay not only for his and his family's pride but also for his workers and, especially, for the community it has served so long with substantial employment, additional locally generated business, and major regional charitable activities. He is the perfect employer and surely would have won Mr. Stone's applause for business responsibility to the community. His neighbors appreciated his generosity and supported his fight to stay in business.

The only problem was that the firm was losing money. Lawrence Garfinckle, a corporate "raider," representing Schumpeter's rational market calculator, specialized in taking "unproductive assets and making them productive." He implored the company's investors—for Jorgenson had been forced to sell shares publicly to survive his last crisis—to be rational and look at the facts. The firm had "bled your money" giving you little return, he asserted, and the owner had no good response. Garfinckle won the critical stockholders takeover vote with many of Jorgenson's friends and neighbors voting their pocketbook against their heart. Ossie, a close friend deserted him at the critical moment. Kate, so trusted that Jorgenson had her represent him before the raider, even marries Garfinckle—in a very rational deal for her. The whole community deserts him. Jorgenson did get $30 million in the deal too when he later sold his shares. Yet, he is so broken and misses his rewarding work and community approval so much, he dies of a broken heart—and leaves most of the estate to his wife who spends it retraining employees in the community who were displaced from their jobs.[9]

Even with $30 million, this does not look like fun but pushing rocks. Jorgenson was the socially conscious employer of every reformist theorist's dreams. But there is no sentiment in the market and even employee-owned firms (e.g., United Airlines) act pretty much like the rest, cutting costs and excess employees when profits are threatened. Union pension plans vote their stock just as ruthlessly as Jorgenson's friends. Still how can one not feel sympathy for Jorgenson, certainly more than for Garfinckle who won the votes and rationalized the firm? Even with his $30 million and the love of his family, Jorgenson was personally destroyed. Would anyone say that fairness required government assistance or some outside welfare to soothe his loss? Does he need more than $30 million, and would it or sympathy even help? The problem was that his work was everything to him and when he lost it he was devastated and died soon thereafter. What is tragic about him—is it not that he had nothing but his work? Do we sympathize because his values did not reach high enough?

The common man philosopher and longshoreman Eric Hoffer argued that America provides a middle solution in giving meaning to work. Auden and Russel speak for the major civilizations, which all were governed (except, he says, Florence) by an aristocracy. Instead, America is run by the masses, who have the freedom to work or not and how hard. Unlike under aristocratic leadership, they do not have to be forced to work. Under freedom, the individual voluntarily prefers to work, not for aristocratic fulfillment or fun but simply to justify his existence as a human being. It was not religion that made him work—certainly not Max Weber's "Protestant ethic," because freedom only really worked in America not in the lands of John Calvin and Martin Luther. They actually tightened a "very lax" Medieval control into a strictness that regulated the "whole conduct" of society through the power of the state, replacing the inefficient social controls of the old church. Rather, it is freedom that "drives" the American to work more effectively than any in the world, not religion. The free individual puts himself "into the hands of a ruthless taskmaster," himself, who makes him work harder than any aristocracy ever dreamed possible. The work of average Americans is not fun, nor even necessarily rewarding, but it is what puts meaning into the free man's life.[10]

A study by the International Labor Organization suggests that Hoffer might be on to something. The average American worked 1,978 hours in the year 2000, up even from earlier years, while work times were actually declining in most other developed nations. Japan, which once logged more hours than the U.S., now worked one month per year less. Hours worked in Europe have declined even more. Indeed, France has forced a European Union maximum number of hours allowed to be worked per week of 35 hours compared to the 40 hour American standard for full-time work. Today, even Germany works three months less per year on average than the U.S. On the other hand, even the hustling Americans are outdone by South Koreans, who work 500 hours more, and Czechs, who work 600 hours more. While both of these latter also are free, other free peoples work much less.[11]

Not only is it difficult to credit hard work to American nationalism alone or to simple freedom, but Crittenden suggests that Hoffer's might simply be a male view. While occupational work may give meaning to most men, business work is not enough for most women. Most women need motherhood and work, according to her, to consider their lives justified. Still, today, 40 percent of women do not participate in the business workforce at all, compared to only 25 percent non-participation for men. On the other hand, while the data show that American women spend significantly less time than men on the job and that many more work only part time, when one includes housework, women work far more hours than men. Men may not place work first either. Polls find that most men say their family is more important than their work. So, there are different types of work and different types of people who may or may not obtain satisfaction from it.[12]

Auden and Russell seem to get little argument against their proposition that philosophical and aristocratic work can be more fulfilling. But all also agree that this highest type of work and reward is unavailable to most people. Ordinary, "mechanical" work, however, does not seem able to be justified simply on its own sake. As Hoffer conceded, freedom only gives "a justification of their existence" to the masses; it does not allow them to "find fulfillment in their work." Fulfillment in inherently non-rewarding work must be justified by some higher good—a philosophy that, unlike Russell's and Auden's or even Hoffer's, justifies work that is not itself worthwhile beyond its practical utility. Philosophy, from Aristotle to the present in the West, does this through the *idea of duty,* which both justifies and dignifies work and the individual's responsibility to it, regardless of its seemingly mundane nature, argues the Christian educator John Henry Newman.[13] Not all people can read Aristotle or Aquinas, but all can get this virtue transmitted to them through some religion, and except for a small minority of intellectuals, most ordinary people have accepted duty this way throughout history. Hoffer is correct that America is unique, but besides being free, it is also the most religious society in the West by far, with the single possible exception of Ireland.[14]

PUSHING ROCKS OR A MEANINGFUL LIFE?

So, is it pushing rocks or can there be a meaningful life?

1. *What is the lesson of 9/11—that duty based in tradition or reason is sometimes required for dangerous work or that the rescuers foolishly sacrificed their lives? Can all the money in the world make people work if they do not see mundane or even dangerous labor as in some manner their duty rather than as simple work that can be shirked or avoided?*
2. *How about the steelworkers and manual workers clearing the site afterwards? What gets them to do the dirty work, much less to sacrifice with long, sometimes uncompensated labor? How much does duty matter even in everyday, repetitive, boring, and stressful work, or—in spite of appearances—is it really meaningful and fun?*
3. *For whatever reason, even in these advanced times, women still do more of the work of raising children, and men still do most of the full-time work. Women are much more likely to choose part-time work, often coordinated with when their children are in school or when children need them. They choose compatible occupations and few find that fighting forces, police, fire-rescue, or even steel-making fits their lifestyles, although a few do. Is this fair, much less fun?*
4. *If men are out having fun and the women are caring for children and only working part time, who will do the dirty, dangerous work? Marx (uncharacteristically) is not clear. Should one teach boys it is fine to live off women's work? Is the stay-at-home father an equally attractive lifestyle? Hoffer and Sommers think that men need work more. Do men have the option, really, that women do? Is that fair?*

5. *The government wants to add more competent baggage screeners. It is boring work. What other than commitment can make workers better screeners? Does anyone seriously think giving the job to better-paid government employees who cannot be fired will help simply because they work for this magic thing called a government or for a bit more money? Must a fully just society be created anew to guarantee fully equal and satisfying work, as Plato, Marx, etc. argued, or must something beyond justify it independently, or does it not matter?*

6. *What does the Jorgenson example demonstrate? Was the nasty market the cause—if so, how can the government solve this market failure for a person with $30 million? Was he selfishly using other people's (stockholders') money to make himself feel good, and did he deserve to lose his company and the fulfillment he derived from it? Or if the market can so easily take these away, does not a person need something beyond money or success or satisfaction to be the higher value?*

7. *But religion, which gives this "higher good" to most people, is precisely what has been rejected by modern rationalism, in Russell, Auden, Nietzsche, Darwin, Freud, Marx, and the rest. Are we back to the beginning of the philosophical debate?*

8. *If religion—especially Western religion broadly defined—is so meaningless, why is there such passion against it? Why is Nietzsche so mad at it?*

9. *Most of the world has some higher explanation—is there some reason for this? Or are we just lifting rocks alone in the universe?*

NOTES

1. Milton Friedman and Anna Jacobson Schwartz, *A Monetary History of the United States* (Princeton: Princeton University Press, 1963), esp. chap. 7. Also see Henry Hazlitt, *The Failure of the New Economics* (Princeton: Van Nostrand, 1959), chap. XXVIII; and Murray Rothbard, *America's Great Depression* (Los Angeles: Nash, 1973), Part III.

2. Milton Friedman, "The Social Responsibility of Business Is to Increase Its Profits," *The New York Times Magazine*, 13 September 1970.

3. Christopher D. Stone, "Why Shouldn't Corporations Be Socially Responsible?" in *Where the Law Ends* (New York: Harper Collins, 1975).

4. W. H. Auden, "Work, Labor and Play," in *A Certain World* (London: Curtis Brown, 1970).

5. Bertrand Russell, "Work," in *The Conquest of Happiness* (London: Liverwright, 1958).

6. David Ewing, "Employee Rights and Duties," in *Freedom Inside the Organization* (New York: Penguin, 1977). Also see Richard Vigilante, *Strike* (New York: Simon & Schuster, 1994).

7. Thomas Friedman, *The Lexis and the Olive Tree* (New York: Random House, 2000).

8. William H. Young, *Ogg and Ray's Introduction to American Government* (New York: Meredith, 1962), chap. 19.

9. Jerry Sterner, *Other People's Money* (New York: Applause Theater Book Publishers, 1989).

10. Eric Hoffer, "The Readiness to Work," *Between the Devil and Dragon* (New York: Harper Collins, 1982).

11. International Labor Organization, <http://laborsta.ilo.org>.

12. Donald J. Devine, *The Political Culture of the United States* (Boston: Little Brown, 1972), 186–87.

13. John Henry Newman, *Idea of a University* (London: Longmans Green, 1852).

14. The Pew Research Center, Pew Global Attitudes Project, December 2002, <http://www.people-press.org> (December 2002).

Chapter Twelve

Values, Citizenship, and the Good Society?

UNIVERSAL, WORLD CITIZENSHIP?

Is it possible that there is some higher universal standard by which all world situations can be judged? The Declaration refers to universal, self-evident truths, but much of the world does not support those values as the higher ones. Can they claim to be universal anyway? Judaism, Christianity, and Islam each proclaim themselves to be universal, although rationalism considers all three parochial and considers itself as the only true universal standard. But there are different rational and scientific theories too, and it is not clear which is universally true, if any. Even if there were a universal standard, how could it be enforced? Or is an appeal to some universal authority possible, or even to something higher?

Malcolm X, at one point, threatened to take the U.S. to the United Nations because his cause could not receive justice from his own parochial nation. He noted how European colonialism oppressed the colored peoples of the world but collapsed under the pressure from universal values represented by the U.N. Why not the same solution for the colored peoples of the United States? Obviously, the U.N. did not take this action against America, but fear of world opinion probably did have an influence on ending segregation there in the 1960s. The U.N. Universal Declaration of Human Rights does provide a certain moral authority that receives some level of world recognition. With the rise of the global market, there has even been a renewed movement of opinion—especially outside of the U.S.—toward forcing the international standards of the United Nations against recalcitrant nations in world courts and to apply world treaties like the Kyoto Protocol on the environment to the richer nations of the West.

Of course, the U.N. is not universal in the sense that it is ruled by a majority of world citizens nor even by all nations speaking with a single voice. There is no direct citizenship in the world body nor even equal power for each nation. The U.N. actually is ruled by its Security Council, which is controlled by five world powers, three (four if one includes Russia) of which are Western. The ruling council does not include a single Muslim nation with permanent membership and a veto, even though by the late 21st century, Islam could be the world's largest universalistic tradition. In important ways, Islam would then be more universal than the U.N. Its universal truth is revealed in great detail and is much more related to problems of everyday life than the Universal Declaration. Moreover, it has direct representation, for every Muslim is a member whatever his nation state. While only believers may be citizens, others may be tolerated, even if not in full communion with the community. In any event, Islam is the only universal ideal that has a clear vision of all peoples ruled directly in one world community, all under one Allah and one law.

The People tradition is the least universalistic in one important sense. All its values are local, residing in one, specific, and concrete people and land. In another sense, however, it is the most universalistic. All nature is one extended family, all of it. All—plants, animals, the dead—are part of one spirit. Citizenship is extended to all—people but also plants, land, animals, and spirits. But is it possible to treat animals and plants equally, even by its own lights? Eagle Man admitted Native Americans shot buffalo but prayed to be "forgiven" for doing so. Forgiveness is a large exception to its own moral rule. Can forgiveness also be given for the much-criticized, ubiquitous strip mall, or even pollution? Likewise, one is to use nature "responsibly," another elastic concept. What happens when people do not, especially migrants from outside? In fact, that is how the tradition of The People has broken down everywhere. The People themselves, almost everywhere, have accepted citizenship in a modern people and most have adopted a universalistic religion. For it is clear that the nation state with its own values and truths has become the dominant modern form of social organization.

A good deal of modern opinion believes that the world's nation states and the once unique cultures that defined those peoples may now be breaking down in the face of overwhelming global forces. Even in the United States, the author John W. Kingdon argues that, yes, the American ideal has been extraordinary successful and has provided a more or less universalistic model for much of the world to emulate. But the world is changing, especially as the result of the universal threats of globalization and world pollution. That is why many peoples and nations are seriously considering the adoption of the Kyoto treaty to drastically limit what the world produces. If this is not done, global warming, ozone depletion, and other environmental problems will presumably flood the world, turn temperate soil to desert, and then destroy all life.[1]

The new worldwide challenges of economic globalism, resource depletion, and environmental hazard should lead Americans to "discover that we cannot afford the luxury of as much individual autonomy as we have been enjoying." There must be more government "coordination and planning" and certain freedoms of citizenship and consumption of goods and services must be given up. "The traditional American emphasis upon individual autonomy and the customary American suspicion of collective action and government initiative may have to bend significantly. It is hard to imagine a way that both allows people to go their own way and still addresses this sort of societal and global problem." The U.S., with 5 percent of the world's population consuming 23 percent of carbon emissions and world goods, especially, will have to cut back on its lifestyle, although perhaps only to European levels, which could become the new world universal standard for economically successful nations. But will even that reduction be enough? Many argue that Europe already consumes too much to sustain a healthy environment.

UNIVERSAL OR NATIONAL STANDARDS?

1. *Is the freedom America enjoys a thing of the past? Does giving the power to national or international authorities offer a good prospect that these governmental institutions can solve the problems? Is a serious Kyoto treaty-type reduction of world production and consumption the only alternative to ecological destruction? Or is there even a serious problem? Many scientists doubt global warming is constant but that it enters cold and warm periods. Others doubt, even if all human production were ended, whether global environmental problems would be significantly affected and suspect that most observed pollution is mainly from natural causes.*

2. *What about the rest of the world? The U.S. might be wealthy enough to stabilize production or even cut it a bit, but most of the world has a very, very long way to go to produce enough even to escape poverty. Can or should they be held back? Should humans be sacrificed for trees or plants? Of course, Kyoto excludes the poorer nations, but then pollution will keep increasing as American standards go down. Should not the environment trump production even in poor countries? Or does production still count too, especially for the very poor?*

3. *How about the reliability of such treaties? In 1972, the Biological Weapons Convention was signed by almost every nation. In 1981, the*

*H'Mong people were attacked by Laos with toxic fungus. In 1984, the So-
viets were caught with large amounts of anthrax and Russia still probably
has the capacity. Sverdlovsk had an anthrax outbreak in 1979. Iraq used
anthrax in its war against Iran from 1980 to 1988 and against the Kurds.
There was the anthrax attack against the U.S. just following 9/11. Given
this record, could one rely upon the UN or a world treaty regime to keep
other countries from cheating on Kyoto, to say nothing about its ability to
manage things like the U.S. anthrax-control program?*

4. *Even those with great compassion for the rest of the world seem reluctant to
accept the reduction in standard of living for the West that would take place
under Kyoto requirements, or even more drastic ones that would truly share
things equally. Worldwide income redistribution would lead to an equal income share of approximately $1,000 per year for all: Would it be politically
possible for the U.S. to adopt this kind of reduction in living standards?*

5. *What would worldwide freedom look like under existing international
standards? The population data from Freedom House suggest the world
norm for individual freedom would be extremely low by American standards. Is that simply an unavoidable cost of universalism, or could standards be increased somehow or another?*

Or are worldwide standards and organizations, at least for the present,
highly unlikely, or even impossible? Whatever the future, today, the nation-
state shows little sign of fading away. The idea of a People, each pursuing its
own version of "self-evident" truths, as the American Declaration put it, is
still the world's dominant form.

SELF-EVIDENT TRUTHS AND AMERICAN CITIZENSHIP

Whatever the merits of the theory, world government has had little popular appeal anywhere. The People tradition may appear passé, but it survives in a
(very) modified form in the modern national state. To almost all in the U.S.,
we are "We the people of the United States of America" with our "more perfect union," based on our own "self-evident" truths, from a Creator, who considers each of his people morally equal and endows them with the right to life,
liberty, and the pursuit of happiness. Most Americans support these national
values, even among most of those who in other ways identify with the universalistic left. Robert Reich, a professor, was Secretary of Labor in the Clinton
Administration and was considered his most liberal cabinet official. Yet, in a
popular book, it is he who argues that there is a common American "morality
tale" that unites its peoples into a common "American" experience and

presents to its people and the world its image of citizenship. While this culture tale has had its negative aspects, it has accounted for much of the nation's success, and it gives it even today a "common hope" that its success will persevere. As befits a liberal intellectual, the "tale" is explicitly labeled "vague" and mythological and based upon "cultural parables" that can and have been interpreted in "multiple manifestations." In short, it is open-ended. But it is sufficient to "summon us to duty and destiny" and provides enough hope for the future so that the American nation will survive and even continue to prosper and, perhaps, even remain a beacon for the remainder of the world.[2]

As is appropriate for his opposite, conservative professor Thomas West defines American values in very concrete terms. He argues that this "tale" is a very tangible one that, from Locke to the Founders, has been based specifically upon the Judeo-Christian vision. It is not vague but is lifted specifically from that tradition and elaborated upon by the early British and American experience and translated into their institutions and rule of law. The "parables" are from Jesus and the prophets and the Founders. Indeed, the whole justifying idea of the Creator is Judeo-Christian in origin. West traces how Locke and the Founders received their ideas and inspiration from the Bible and its religion by citing their concurring views rather extensively. He concedes that the vision rests upon reason as well as revelation, but he sees both as rising from the same tradition. The American culture even includes the value of toleration of other beliefs, an "old truth" practiced early and relayed through Locke to all America. All of these precisely define the duties of American citizenship, at least to this representative of the American right. To him, belief in these values must be widely supported among the population if the enterprise called the U.S. is to continue to succeed. Belief cannot be vague but it need not be unanimous, for tolerance allows for some exceptions, as long as these are not so numerous that there are not enough supporting citizens left to uphold the major institutions.[3]

As Reich argued, to a great extent the values are shared by both American conservatism and liberalism—although both he and West would agree the differences in emphasis matter greatly and that the way each is ranked in importance can be critical to social happiness. Yet, what is agreed upon is considered essential to justify America's Constitutional regime and can even be considered America's vision for how any world society could be best constituted.

CAN AMERICAN CITIZENSHIP BE CONSIDERED UNIVERSAL CITIZENSHIP?

1. *What is self-evident in the American tradition is that all men are created equal and endowed by a Creator with certain unalienable rights and that*

among them is the right to life, liberty, and the pursuit of happiness. From Locke onward, liberty, family, private property, and limited government have constituted the core values. But are these universal desires or even the ones that still motivate most Americans?

2. *What could rival these values, The People tradition? Most Native Americans today are Christians, as was Seattle, and support the values of the Declaration. Polls not surprisingly show that Islam, Hinduism, and the other major traditions have few adherents. Surveys show only a small portion of the population admit they are secular, but leave unclear whether secularism, self-interest, and fun might really rival the "self-evident truths" as the values that actually motivate Americans. Is fun really the American religion?*

3. *Kingdon presents a very sophisticated alternative to the Declaration values, what may be called the "half-European solution." Globalization and environmental problems now require much more government regulation of property and liberty, something closer to the way Europe operates today. But estimates are that Europe (including Russia) will decline from 727 million today to 556 million—a 24 percent decline or 171 million fewer Europeans by 2050. Actual population declines are already evident in AUSTRIA, Belarus, Bulgaria, Czech Republic, Estonia, Hungary, ITALY, Latvia, Lithuania, Moldova, Romania, Russia, Slovenia, SPAIN, SWEDEN and Ukraine. BELGIUM, Croatia, FINLAND, GERMANY, and GREECE will follow in the next few years. Is Europe a more realistic model, or will there even be a Europe as we know it in 100 years?*

4. *Might the traditional American self-evident truths still provide the superior universal model for the world to follow?, The World Bank data on prosperity, liberty, property, and the rule of law suggests its continuing attractiveness to new peoples like the Central European nations (not capitalized above) which have recently slipped the Soviet yoke and demonstrate more vitality? Or can these "truths" not be widely accepted and adopted, and so are unsustainable for most nations over time, as the data (so far) also confirm?*

5. *Reich's "morality tale" has a secular ring and is self-admittedly vague and mythical. Can such a tale hold people to their duty over the long haul? It is fine for those who already have an attachment to these myths, but what about new entrants and the next generation? How can one teach, much less develop moral commitment to a tale that is admittedly less than real? Or is it in fact so powerful that it is self-sustaining?*

6. *The values that Professor West identifies as critical to the continuing success of the U.S. are concrete rather than vague, specified in the Bible and organized in churches and other houses of worship, and translated into the*

Declaration, Constitution, government, and secular institutions. He also claims that the Judeo-Christian and American tales are true. But what about those from different traditions? Since he accepts that the government must be secular, what happens if a large group rejects this tradition? Of course, polls show that fewer than a tenth of the population are from outside the Judeo-Christian tradition, and few reject the institutional values, but what about the future? Or is one-tenth already sufficient to undermine legitimacy?

TOLERANCE AND VALUES

Is Religion Antagonistic to Tolerance?

The question to Professor West is, how can he expect general belief in the values of one religious tradition and still have tolerance for others, a value he also specifies as important to the American vision? How can a religion that believes its values are superior to others support a free, democratic state open to other faiths? Certainly, some religions would find this difficult—for example, Islam unless it significantly loosens its attachment to the state. But Michael Seube, in the leading article in the prestigious *Washington Post* Sunday Opinion section, proclaimed that religion generally fosters intolerance, not just Islam. Tolerance and separation of powers—even of church and state—were inventions of the secular Enlightenment, he argued, as it weakened and then replaced religion to create the modern secular West. Christian fundamentalists "know the Bible better than they know Voltaire or Rousseau, Gibbon or Hume…but they laid the foundation, even in spirited disagreement with one another, for separation of church and state, for freedom of speech and worship, for tolerance and for the simple injunction to live and let live." Contrary to Professor West, religion had to be supplanted by secularism to produce the modern, tolerant state.[4]

Yet, it is Seube who is confused. Voltaire (1694–1778), Rousseau (1712–1778), Gibbon (1734–1794), and Hume (1711–1776) come very late to the game. The tolerant, secular government supported by religion—but neutral toward any individual one—was invented much earlier. A recent book claims that tolerance was first practiced by Islam in Moorish Spain. However, the author concedes there were limitations to that tolerance—that the other "peoples of the book" were first and foremost not allowed to proselytize, could build no new churches or synagogues, display no symbols like crosses, and had to pay a tax not applicable to Muslims. She documents that Jews generally accepted the limitations and were successful in adapting to the Muslim system, often achieving positions of great influence.[5] However, these were restrictions Christians could not accept. The last instruction by Jesus to his followers was to preach his doctrine to the whole world and baptize all who would accept it. Christians who followed this commandment of their founder were subject to death under the Moors and, therefore, were not in fact tolerated in their Spain. Christians were either forced to convert, pressured into it for the rewards citizenship—which was otherwise denied—could provide, or marginalized.

As noted earlier, the historian Lord Acton concluded that the first free, tolerant society in the world was Christian Maryland—with George Calvert's charter of 1632 giving the vote to all freemen upon settlement in 1634 and the formal passage of the Toleration Act in 1649—long before Voltaire even was born. Lord Baltimore's contemporary Charles II of Britain tried this solution too, but both attempts were ultimately overturned by the Glorious Revolution. William Penn, however, took up their mantle under the Quaker Christian guise, and his successful implementation of it in Pennsylvania predated all of the secularists too. Even Locke was relatively late (1632–1704), but it was he who preceded and inspired his fellow Enlightenment thinkers into supporting tolerance, although he was less successful in implementing it than was Penn. Unlike his fellow Enlightenment figures, however, Locke was a believing Christian as were the other leaders of the early movement toward toleration.[6] Moreover, "render to Caesar" was from the very beginning of Western civilization, to say nothing of Samuel. As early as Attila's invasion of Italy in A.D. 452, the church was separate from the state and it was Pope Leo I who saved Rome from destruction in the church's name, not the state's.

Rousseau's Tolerance

The only attribute the thinkers cited by Suebe had in common, as he alludes, is that they disliked Christianity and wanted to get it out of government. But most, and particularly Rousseau, did not support separation of church and state. In fact, he complained that Christianity separated powers—that was what he did not like about it. Separate loyalties could lead to disunity in the state. The great student of the rise of capitalism, Max Weber, found that Medieval control was "lax," and it was not until the Middle Age institutions were successfully challenged by the rise of the modern state that state and church were united in most of Europe. As the European states manipulated the unrest of the Reformation, on both Protestant and Catholic sides, state power was added to religious views and caused the great intolerance, wars, and disruption that followed. In its wake, later Enlightenment thinkers recognized toleration as a solution.[7] As Acton emphasized, this applied particularly to England, which retained more of the Medieval mindset and institutions than the others and was able to transfer these ideas of limited government to America before Britain itself became part of the problem too, as the Declaration documented.

As Seube notes, Rousseau proposed a purely secular tolerance as his solution. But it is an interesting type of toleration. It consists of a seven point logical argument:[8]

1. All people need values to provide meaning and order for their lives.
2. Governments require people who hold moral values, so they will not fight constantly with each other but will obey proper laws derived from the general will.
3. "True" Christianity is a possible moral system to support such a society but it "preaches only servitude and dependence" so that its followers are "made to be slaves," not real citizens.
4. Much of actual Christianity is "clearly bad," not worth serious consideration, because it "destroys social unity" with its dual claims of loyalty to both church and state.
5. Therefore, the "sovereign should fix the articles" of a new civic religion. The government should create a moral system that is useful to them in governing and in producing law-abiding citizens but should not call it a religion. It should teach it as a "social sentiment" that all decent people must hold to be good citizens. If some people cannot accept the sentiment, they cannot be good citizens and must be banished.
6. In sum, "tolerance should be given to all religions that tolerate others, so long as their dogmas contain nothing contrary to the duties of citizenship."
7. While he does not emphasize it again at this point in his argument, the argument of number four above is that actual Christian dogma destroys social unity and thus is "contrary to the duties of citizenship," so actual Christianity in fact would not be tolerated.

So this theorist living in the center of Europe proposes to tolerate everything but actual Christianity, and we are supposed to take this seriously as tolerance? In other words, this is a fraud. Rousseau does not tolerate what he firmly dislikes, Christianity as it in fact works in the real world. He does not much like it in its "true" form either, since that supposedly promotes servitude. Either way, Christianity divides power and makes the state less efficient. Tolerance or, better, religious freedom in the American sense is more robust than Rousseau's secular tolerance. While the later insists upon a single "social sentiment" for the community, the former follows the Federalist and allows different fundamental religious beliefs—indeed, the multiple Christian denominations virtually demand it—as long as people obey the law and support the self-evident truths. True, tolerance in the West has limits. Those who violate the self-evident truths of protecting life, promoting liberty under rules of law, and allowing others to pursue their happiness—they break the social contract. Does anyone actually tolerate everything? In the modern, secular U.S., many who consider themselves tolerant of everything are righteous in banning tobacco or forbidding animal hunting. To the secularist, Madonna the Material Girl is tolerated, publicly promoting Mary Madonna of Christ is called intolerance, unless her image is smeared in feces, when it can be featured in a government-supported art gallery. A crucifix of Christ cannot be tolerated by government unless it is put in urine by an artist, who then can receive a government grant for it. This is value neutrality? Can all values be relative? But if all values are relative, they are equal. Are Hitler, Stalin, and bin Laden really just as good as George Washington? Really?

By its nature, government sets rules and these are based on values. Even when neutral toleration and freedom are put into government rules in a limited way—as the West actually has attempted to do with a neutral rule of law—that itself is a value judgment, as is preference for rule of law itself. Peoples create some legal order that incorporates their values and those that do not follow it are prosecuted to some degree or another, even if there is substantial room for toleration and freedom too. People are tolerated if they follow those laws, whether secular or religious in origin. Professor West argues that the American solution is to set general rules of law against injury of one's neighbor, based upon the values of its universal religious tradition, for a limited number of things and then all other things can be tolerated under a system of liberty that also allows an active religious life and a free economic system. But must not deciding what is allowed and what is not allowed be determined by some set of values, rather than by some specious and nonexistent neutrality?

WHAT IS AMERICAN CITIZENSHIP?

State Participation?

Within some set of values, a certain neutrality is possible, although it is difficult to create and maintain such institutions. The rule of law is one such device devised within the West that was transferred to the United States. As the World Bank study referred to earlier demonstrates, this has been difficult for the rest of the world to imitate. Several sources have been cited to suggest that the rule is even in some decline within the U.S. in recent years, replaced by specific preferences for favored social welfare interests. The market, too, is such a device, but again, it has been difficult to create and maintain in most of the world. In the West, the welfare state has limited the invisible hand of free trading supported by property law with presumably neutral decisions by supposedly objective experts so that the state can provide greater fairness than the market for ends like justice, equality, and toleration. The problem for this new institution has been, as Myrdall recognized from the beginning, that the welfare state receives its legitimacy from its democracy value, that it will reflect the people's will. But what happens when the people will not support the experts to do what is necessary to create social justice? Should policy follow what the people value or what the government experts believe they need?

Former Harvard University president Derek Bok recently confronted this old problem and attempted a new resolution for today's welfare state. He supported the continuing need for an active democratic national government "where citizens come to depend upon the State to meet so many of their needs." But he was deeply concerned that most people today do not think this large "government performs" well and do not trust it with enough power to be effective. What could be done? What about making the government more democratic? He reviewed several possible proposals but concluded that increased democratic control seems impossible when Americans are willing to invest only "modest effort" in greater participation. But they are also unwilling to limit democratic means such as primaries and initiatives or to give more power to unelected experts in the executive, the judiciary, or independent agencies. He suggested giving more power to citizen lobbies and advocacy groups as expert substitutes or lobbyists for the people, but recognized that these were not the people directly but were only surrogates, and they "cannot do everything" in the people's name in any event

Bok concludes that the national government will continue to dispense most welfare through decisions by national experts but that the people will not continue to support the large role required unless there is more popular participation. But people are unwilling to become more involved. He resolves his twin concerns by calling for citizen participation through additional citizen education and more knowledge about government rather than direct participation in decision-making. Indirect participation may not be ideal, but it does involve the people and is the most that can be expected to provide democratic legitimacy for an effective state in the modern world.[9]

Is Neutral Citizenship Enough?

It is not clear what should be taught in this citizenship education. What is obvious is that the modern, secular welfare state attempts to be neutral and ignore values in this process and, especially, to avoid religion in its teachings. The good citizen is mainly expected to follow the law—to defer to the neutral experts, to allow them to do their work and not to act in ways that will frustrate their governance. Yet, is neutral, passive citizenship enough to sustain a government based upon consent? Aristotle demands action for behavior to be considered moral at all. For him, education is not enough to qualify for good citizenship. Symbolic participation is passive. The Soviet Union proved that a passive citizenry relying on experts cannot maintain order over a long period of time even in a repressive regime. In a democracy, governing authorities cannot plan or do everything but must rely upon active citizen participation at least to keep order in daily social interactions, as well as to train and nurture the succeeding generations. This involved participation requires that they have some non-neutral, interior moral ideas that tell them how to act, as Rousseau recognized—even if it is only from a civil religion—if society is to function at all. Where governments are limited in power, as they are in the West, they must rely even more upon citizen-generated active morality to make markets, families, and voluntary associations work.

As a factual matter, for the most part, the morality relied upon in the West to keep basic social order has come from religion. Christianity did not explicitly plan for any particular form of constitution, for freedom in the modern sense, much less for a market, or for a limited government based upon consent. These developed as the result of its wariness about government interfering with the rights of its churches. Limiting government power and expanding the scope of freedom came as the unplanned result of the tension between its organized religions and other independent and local institutions and the state over centuries of lived experience. As far as adopting the secular state religion option proposed by Rousseau is concerned, Voltaire gave the historic riposte. Although a great opponent of religion, he was skeptical about too easy solutions. Voltaire is reputed to have replied to a student who proposed to create a civic religion: Fine, all you have to do is be killed and rise on the third day to give your civic religion the necessary credibility to challenge Christianity's claimed historical fact. Actually, the solution was tried in Revolutionary France, including abolishing Christianity and even changing the Christian calendar. However, Napoleon was forced to reinstitute both religion and calendar only a few years later.[10]

Religion in Modern Times

Religion may not be quite as dead as has been predicted for the last 300 years by these Enlightenment philosophers. Islam, certainly, is growing. The best estimate is that it will increase by 100 percent in population in the next fifty years to reach 2 billion people. In contrast, Western secularism is not replacing itself in population growth. Christianity overall is projected to increase by

50 percent. That is only half the rate of Islam, but would still leave Christianity at 3 billion adherents, one billion greater than the Muslim total. While Christianity is decreasing in the West because secularism is advancing, Christianity is increasing in Latin America, Africa, and Asia. Indeed, Christians in South America (480 million), Africa (360 million), and Asia (313 million) already outnumber Christians in Europe (560 million, at least in name) and North America (260 million) by 1.2 billion to 800 million. The question is how much of what is called the Western tradition will continue or transfer with the religion to the other continents?

In any event, today, Americans do get their values from traditional religion, primarily Christianity, with eight in ten identifying with it as their creed. The state, in turn, is secular and neutral between religions, but it relies upon beliefs taken from the Judeo-Christian tradition to sustain its ordinary social life and its legal code. Christianity and Judaism insist people are fundamentally equal—morally—and that all will be ultimately accountable for how they were responsible for their neighbor. Even Greece saw people as fundamentally unequal—that is why Plato went to such lengths in the Republic and why Aristotle thought equality was impossible. Who says people are equal in any way—moral, legal, or social—with any authority? Religious beliefs say so in the American setting. Its government might, in some abstract way, be able to sustain order without people feeling a religious responsibility to be good to one's neighbor, but how? This feeling of neighborliness might conceivably have come from some other source, but in fact, it did not. It is the Judeo-Christian idea of the Creator that tells them (or many of them) to have pity on their neighbor (at least a bit), which has been demonstrated from their response to the World Trade Center attack to their generous daily lives. In fact, polls do confirm that very large majorities of Americans do and should trust their neighbor and believe they must cooperate to some degree with him and her if there is to be a rewarding social life.

The degree of religiosity in the United States has always been a mystery to secularists, who expected that it would have expired decades ago, especially in its most economically advanced country. All of the polls demonstrate that over 90 percent of Americans believe in God and only 4 percent or so do not, with 4 percent not sure. Two-thirds say religion is "very important" to them and another one-fifth say it is fairly important. Only 10 percent say they never pray. A substantial 71 percent say they "belong" to a church or house of worship. Self-reported weekly church or religious attendance is about 40 percent, matching the number of Americans who watch the Super Bowl, the largest secular attraction—but religion does it every week. And attendance at church has stayed about the same since the 1930s, according to the polls.[11] Although the Putnam data suggest it is less active participation, so is watching football, and that is only once a year. Indeed, Putnam convincingly demonstrates the overwhelming importance of religious participation to social and political participation in general. Religious participation is the best predictor of participation in governmental or political activities, neighborliness, and voluntary association work. It is difficult to believe that this high attraction to neighborliness and religion does not in some degree explain its likewise unique attachment to limited government, popular consent, rule of law, property, and the market. Other types of governments have different requirements, but the Western combination has been quite successful.

Or Is Civic Activity Required?

To Aristotle, private moral action is simply not enough. There must also be active participation with fellow members of the community, including in the activities of its government, which decides many of the most important things in life. Is this possible in the modern nation state? First of all, it is far away and so large, how can a single citizen have effect? Indeed, the Marquis de Condorcet demonstrated mathematically that participation in a large national government was irrational for any individual in terms of his small proportionate influence, incidentally costing him his head during the French Revolution.[12] Even government by national referenda would be manipulated by question wording and the like, which would have to be determined by government experts. While the welfare state has the best intentions for involving citizens, in fact, its commitment to expertise must discourage it. Independent citizen activity must sometimes conflict with expert plans. Citizen participation that has citizens actually making decisions could get in the way, and that is why symbolic participation is deemed more important.

However irrational—and only half of citizens do vote in the U.S.—ballots do determine who will lead and those leaders do make national policy. But the voters do not set the policy directly, as Madison intended by instituting representation and separation of powers. Alexis de Tocqueville, however, described a means in the early United States that did give ordinary citizens a major role in setting policy. It was an arrangement that gave most of the governing function to the local community with a national government that concerned itself only with truly countrywide issues. While national government was almost absent in the local community and had very little effect upon their normal, daily lives, the people held it in very high regard. Active citizen participation took place in local governments and in voluntary associations, which were the predominant form of government in the U.S. into the 20th century. While many market developments since then have altered things immeasurably, most of the change from local to national power was the result of a political program.

The early progressives set out to reduce independent local power because divided power frustrated their plan to reform the whole society through larger-scale national and state governments. That plan to centralize power has been very successful over the last century, where national and state governments have grown at the expense of local control. Local government represented a majority of all government spending in 1902 but was cut in half, to represent only one quarter of government resources by the 1990s. There was only half the number of local governments per population at the end of the century as there was at the beginning. The decline in independent school districts was even more dramatic. The number of separate schools systems was reduced from 127,000 independent districts in 1902 to only 14,000 today. These results were explicit parts of the progressive program to decrease parochial power and transfer it to national experts who could plan more effectively for society.[13]

To de Tocqueville, true democratic citizenship required that ordinary citizens have the power to affect their everyday civic life, which they could only have locally. Most people, in fact, act only there. Markets and globalism generally may set the broad economic framework, but local customs and norms provide much of the context to daily life. As he demonstrated, when these local relationships are strong, the national government too can be supported more highly for the functions that it must perform. National citizenship participation for average citizens only makes sense in voting and obeying commands, but local citizenship can be meaningful in many areas of societal importance if it is delegated sufficient power and responsibility, while limiting its power to expropriate property or trespass civil rights. The only growing local government in the U.S. today is actually private, as people attempt to replace the formal local government denied to them by law with private alternatives such as community associations, amenity cooperatives, edge cities, business districts, street-closing regimes, and many more. Private voluntary residential community associations alone—which now hold more people than the nation's central cities—can and do perform almost every local government function except sentence people to jail.

As a result of a renewed sense of the importance of local involvement, the "civil society" movement to revitalize local community is one of the strongest movements in the nation today. While poll data show that the popular support necessary for such a recovery of local and voluntary power is still alive in modern America, an enormous amount of the work of the last one hundred years would have to be reversed to revive the local government and voluntary association citizenship that de Tocqueville so admired about America.[14]

THE INDIVIDUAL AND CITIZENSHIP

Individual Action

A famous social science experiment by psychologist Stanley Milgram demonstrated that, when people are on their own, they will often not raise or apply their own values but will follow the nearest available authority figure — with, in the modern era, scientists playing the role of the old-time witch doctor — up to and including inflicting gratuitous pain on innocent fellow citizens. Individuals — for that is what people in an experiment are, all alone with the scientist manipulating them — will not act on their values unless they feel comfortable with them, receiving outside social support for them. In the experiment, the scientific testers in their neutral uniforms told the subjects to keep turning a simulated pain dial on their human experimental subjects to electrically shock them until they "learned," even if this resulted in severe pain. A majority of students in the experiment followed — some reluctantly, some willingly — the experimental leader's instructions to inflict significant pain.[15] Individuals left alone can be swayed by circumstances or clever argument — the demagogues Plato and Madison feared in democracies — which can overcome even their pity. Is not the only way to give assurance and backbone to ordinary, non-philosophical people through some type of organized social value support, most often by associations and religion in particular, as even non-believers like Hayek believed? Or is that all just softness and myth and lies, as Nietzsche taught? Or, incredibly, because it is so essential to good social life, could it be true, at least in some sense or another?

Author Gertrude Himmelfarb is suspicious of the "agreement" in America today over the need for "civil society." As we have seen, while both types of civic involvement can be defended, there is a great difference between national symbolic participation and local civic action. There is apparent agreement, she maintains, only because people are afraid to confront the difficult decision to debate the morality of real behavior in society. "Civic society" is an excuse not to defend the historical tradition and its values, and it is a pretext not to provide a systematic analysis and an alternative. It is hard to argue with her that, today, there is an inability to stigmatize any behavior as wrong in America. There is an unwillingness to seriously confront substantial issues about proper behavior in social situations or to demand any necessary changes in people's behavior. Institutions use the neutral language of sociology to talk of "dysfunctional" families when the need is to teach the "vigorous" virtues that would result in strong families and communities, she argues — "adventurousness, energy, independence, courage."[16]

Instead, American education—as set by the leadership of the National Education Association and the education colleges—teach that "adjustment" is the highest value, following Freud, and de-emphasize heroism or even courage, as Jenny Lyn Bader has demonstrated. Its mostly women leaders and teachers, Himmelfarb says, fear any demonstration of aggression and do everything to suppress it—naturally mostly in boys, as Christiana Hoff Summers argued also. Intellectuals generally tend to support the official view of education, and a number, like Nietzsche and Rousseau, go further to detest traditional Western values, especially Christian religion. As Bader argues, the popular media are especially effective scoffers at the heroic way of life, very much including religious obligation. But the reaction to the 9/11 attack found that these were still essential symbols supporting American social life, as demonstrated by the omnipresent religious iconology used during the memorial gatherings to celebrate both life and the courage of resistance and recovery. To restore true citizenship, Himmelfarb concludes, it will require a "tougher civil society than that envisaged by many who speak in its name." It will need to "stigmatize" bad behavior as well as reward good behavior. This is more necessary in a free society, like the U.S., "for the more effective the social sanctions, the less need there is for the legal and penal sanctions of the state."

Are the vigorous virtues like courage what is most lacking in modern America? It does seem awfully easy to use freedom to just stand back and let the heroes, saints, princes, supermen, and experts do it all. But that makes individuals simply the passive subjects of these rulers, which is what most of the world's population were for most of its history. Aristotle taught that virtue requires action under any circumstances, but Lehrman argues that, in a democracy, moral action must come from all citizens, or almost all. Do Americans today even have the moral courage to teach and defend the values polls show that they, themselves, supposedly believe?[17] Can Americans even stigmatize what they themselves define as bad behavior like stealing and infliction of pain, even to their own children? Americans say they believe that both a father and mother are best for rearing children. But do they have the courage to teach their children that this is how they should live their lives—especially if they are from a single family themselves, where their mother performed heroically, as was the case with the author's own upbringing? They believe that children are good and need their mothers and fathers living with them to nurture them as they grow. Do they have the courage to teach that parents need to stay together when things get tough, if at all possible?

Americans believe that neighbors are morally equal and must not be injured and even deserve pity because they believe their Creator commanded them to act that way. Do they have the courage to demand that behavior from their children, or from themselves? They believe that people are morally equal in the eyes of the law and should be treated equally before it because they were created equal. They believe that individuals need social groups like family, community, religion, associations, and corporations to live to the fullest and that an individual cannot just look out for himself. They believe that there is a need for a protecting military and to support its unique values and traditions. They believe that freedom and the market are just and work best for human prosperity, at least better than anything else we know about. They believe that local knows best, but that nation states like the United States are the only proven defense for their values, so that both are needed. They believe that divided government may look messy sometimes, but it has worked longer and better for justice than any alternative. They believe that work comes before play and that courageous action to assist neighbor or community is sometimes demanded. But will they—or you—have the courage to teach and live up to the values they and you claim to support?

Is the West Worth Saving?

Are the West—including its protecting nation, the United States—and its values worth saving? Strangely, the answer is pretty much up to you, to all of us. If these are to endure, several things must happen and it is not at all clear that they will. The most certain requirement is, no civilization can survive without people. The West would have to achieve a birthrate of 2.1 (or so) children per childbearing-aged woman to even replace itself. Based on extrapolating existing statistics, that seems impossible for Europe and improbable for the United States, especially for its native-born population. Does it matter whether American women can find the courage to give birth—and it does take courage and commitment—or men stay and nurture their children and assist their wives, especially as they age? Actually, the recently released National Center for Health Statistics data for the year 2000 show that, for the first time in thirty years, the U.S. birth rate may have equaled, exactly, the rate necessary to replace the population, and the divorce rate declined, if only marginally.[18] Are the trends reversing?

If the population can be sustained, what goals and values are necessary for its continued success: Glaucon's everyone for themselves, Plato's guaranteed fairness for all, Marx's full social equality for all, or Locke's rule of law based upon liberty, separation of powers, and consent? Is the Lockean value formula enacted by the Founders essential to future prosperity, or is it now old-fashioned as Kingdon suggests, or does it not matter? If society's goal is to be changed from liberty to guarantee equal results to all, how is this to be accomplished without undermining the other values? If the idea is to take it from the rich and redistribute it, at some point resentment, as in much of South America, encourages coups by the wealthy and upper middle classes, often allied with the military. If the new goal is to include making play and leisure the highest values, how long do the heroic professions like the military retain their support for the endeavor? Demands for justice must end somewhere — unless Plato's Republic is the solution — or liberty of citizens is curtailed as in Plato's Republic and the government is overwhelmed by too many conflicting claims, as leading thinkers today from progressives like Dionne and Walzer to conservatives like Meyer and Kristol agree.

Weinberg, a serious critic on the left, is not optimistic that the people will accept a limited definition of what is fair or just or what a democratic government should be able to do to achieve it. Can an American population that Bok finds unwilling to participate be willing to give the experts the necessary power to make the decisions for them? Or is granting the power to far away experts too passive? Is active participation in local or voluntary decision-making for their community and associations required? Is this still possible in a globalized world? Freedom requires self-restraint, but is a morality of self-restraint — whether Judeo-Christian or from the Declaration or even of the secular "morality tale" — passé in the modern world of self-reliance? Is it a world of easy manipulation of peoples by leaders — as the Milgram experiment suggests — or is it an age of anarchy where no "protecting strata" of military, church, or democratic leaders can gain enough prestige to maintain a government even of limited powers? Could a renewed commitment to duty change this? Or is it all power, myth, and lifting rocks?

As Dorothy found when she pulled back the magic cover from Oz's Wizard, there is nothing behind the big social institutions but ordinary people. Is it necessary for most or all the members of society to accept limits on their own power and courageously accept moral responsibility themselves, perhaps fortified by their belief in a Creator? Is that what the preceding generations did to pass to us the great wealth, order, freedom, and decent social harmony we mostly enjoy today? Is the future in everyone's hands, each one of us, even in the face of our own powerful passion to first please ourselves? If so, the responsibility is overwhelming. No wonder so many fear to grasp it. But that has consequences too. As the philosopher Edmund Burke put it: "All that is needed for the triumph of evil is that good men [and women] do nothing."

NOTES

1. John W. Kingdon, *America the Unusual* (New York: St. Martins, 1998).
2. Robert Reich, *Tales of ca New America* (New York: Times Books, 1987).

3. Thomas West, "The Founders Embrace of Rights and Duties," in *Witherspoon Fellowship Lectures* (Washington, D.C.: Family Research Council, 2001). Also see Michael Novak, *On Two Wings: Humble Faith and Common Sense* (New York: Encounter, 2001).

4. Michael Seube, *The Washington Post*, 21 October 212001, B1 and B4. Also see Fareed, especially 150.

5. Maria Rosa Menolal, *The Ornament of the World* (Boston: Little Brown, 2002), 72–73. Because they could not enter the military without converting, Christians could not even hold temporary title to land. See Lord Kinross, *The Ottoman Centuries* (New York: Harper-Collins, 2000), 33–36 and Amin Maalouf, *The Crusades Through Arab Eyes* (New York: Shoeken Books, 1984), 263. Kinross mentions a "rough" separation of church and state under the Ottomans (205) but two things are clear. One, it is an administrative distinction under the Sultan's total control; i.e., the state is unquestionably unified and on top. The caliphs were either in charge (rarely) or were under control of a sultan or vizier. Second, there is no ulema challenge to the state. At best, reforms were occasionally delayed, obstructed or undermined when a ruler was weakened and liable to one of the frequent coups; (see, ff. 461. In 1,500 years, there is no direct challenges to or refusals of authority by authoritative religious leaders equivalent to Ambrose, Thomas a Becket, William Tyndale, Thomas More, St. Joan, Martin Luther, Agnes, Jeremiah, Isaiah, Nathan, etc. (with a very few possible Shi'ah exceptions for short periods of time, before a new lay leader assumed absolute control). And there were no other institutions than the mosque, which was simply a place to pray rather than an organization, that had a moral basis to survive much less to compete against the central state for any period of time. As Zakaria put it, the problem was the reverse, anyone could speak for Islam so no one could do so authoritatively —which led sometimes to anarchy but more often to strong state control. "With no central religious authority, the supremacy of state over church—which arose in Europe as a result of the religious wars—has always existed in the lands of Islam," 147.

6. Devine, "John Locke," passim.

7. See Eric Hoffer, "The Readiness to Work," *Between the Devil and Dragon* (New York: Harper Collins, 1982).

8. Jean-Jacques Rousseau, "The Social Contract," in *The Social Contract and Discourses and Other Essays*, trans. G. D. H. Cole (New York: Everyman's Library, 1950), passim.

9. Derek Bok, "Democracy in the 21st Century: Easing Political Cynicism with Civic Involvement," in *The Trouble with Government* (Cambridge, Mass.: Harvard University Press, 2001), 10–14 and 398-402.

10. On the need for religion for a free society, see Hayek, *The Fatal Conceit*, 137.

11. "Believer Nation," *Public Perspective* (May/June 2000), 24; Pew, *American Views on Religion*, 67–71; "The New Spirituality," *The Washington Times*, 12 April 2000, A12. For the stability of these attitudes over time, see Barry A. Kosmin and Seymour P. Lachman, *One Nation Under God* (New York: Harmony Books, 1993, and Devine, *Political Culture*, 222–28. Even the media has increased church attendance from 14 to 30 percent since the 1980s: Suzanne Fields, "Journalists and the 'New Time' Religion," *The Washington Times*, 18 May 2000, A21. Even one-third

those Americans who tell pollsters they have "no religion" also say they are religious in their outlook; see Ariela Keysar, Egon Mayer and Barry A. Kosmin, "No Religion," *Public Perspective* (January/February 2003), 29.

12. Gordon Tullock, "Theoretical Forerunners," in James M. Buchanan and Gordon Tullock, *The Calculus of Consent* (Ann Arbor, Mich.: University of Michigan Press, 1962), 322–40.

13. Donald Devine, "A Tocquevillean Response to Globalization and Community Decay," *ACU Policy Views*, February 2001.

14. Robert A. Nisbet, *The Quest for Community* (New York: Oxford University Press, 1953), chap. 3.

15. Stanley Milgram, "The Perils of Obedience," *Obedience To Authority* (New York: Harper Collins, 1974).

16. Gertrude Himmelfarb, "Second Thoughts on Civil Society," *The Weekly Standard*, 9 September 1996.

17. Zogby International Poll on National Guidelines for Sexuality and Character Education issued by the Medical Institute for sexual Health, *The Washington Times*, 15 February 2003, A5.

18. National Center for Health Statistics, at <http://www./cdc.gov/nchs>.

Chapter Thirteen

Epilogue

It has been the theme of this book that the uniqueness of the Western vision comes from its way of looking at the world, the institutions it developed to actualize that understanding, and the moral propositions it derived from both. Starting in Jerusalem, it saw its world as made by a rational and caring Creator who designed a vast "array" of reality and formed humanity into His own image. Consequently, His people were rational also and tasked with responsibility for that diverse reality.[1] In Athens, too, that creation was perceived as both material and spiritual, divine and human, body and soul, good and bad, ideal and concrete, reflective and active, individual and communal—where "all data harmonize" under God into the responsible individual life and the balanced social polity.[2] As the vision was consolidated in Christian Europe, its social life was understood as being based upon both reason and tradition, natural law and God's law, state and society, individual freedom and community responsibility, family obligation and property ownership, law and settled beliefs, popular consent and government power.[3] At the time it was transferred to America, the vision remained a complex one, one that was ordered but included division, balance, and synthesis as major attributes.[4]

For most of the past, including in Greece and Rome, social life consisted solely of the state and its subjects—until a voice pierced time and separated state from society, Caesar from God. It was the Christian Church that "was the first major institution in history that was independent of temporal authority and willing to challenge it."[5] Over time other institutions won independent power and also were able to challenge and balance it: lords, knights, squires, parishes, guilds, cities, businessmen, corporations, and local, regional, and national associations and—finally—common citizens with independent property

159

and power of their own. As Lord Acton argued, division of power was the means used in the West to translate the duality, synthesis, and harmony of the ideal into concrete social practice.[6] Before the European religious wars of the 17th century arrested this diffusion of power with the development of the modern, centralized, and secular state, this decentralized institutional form transfused with religious imagery was transferred to America, but in a less calcified form, more open to change. It all became real in its Constitutional checks and balances and its Tocquevillean multiplicity of vibrant local community and private social life.

As this Western vision was transferred to America, it found its moral voice in the Declaration of Independence, which summarized its national proposition: "We hold these truths to be self-evident, that all men are created equal, that they are endowed by their Creator with certain unalienable rights, that among these are life, liberty and the pursuit of happiness." Concretely, the theme acted itself out as the history of the United States of America. As de Tocqueville noted, America's uniqueness lay in the fact that it relied more upon voluntary citizenship and less upon national government than any previous type. But this fact that the people handled problems individually and locally paradoxically resulted in higher support for the national institutions than in any other nation.

The idea of centralization, with a single source of power residing in the state rather than multiple centers of power, eventually made its way to America. While it was resisted longer and made less progress against the traditional values and disbursed institutions of its origin, by the mid-20th century, the national government became the principal means of raising revenue and the ultimate source of most social and economic law and regulation. Checks and balances were weakened as national powers grew relative to state and local ones and expert bureaucratic and judicial powers dominated those of elected officials. While an occasional Supreme Court ruling might partially and temporarily support some state, local, or private power against the national government, this was very much a national decision. As a matter of course, local, state, and private action was made subject to whatever regulations the national Congress or bureaucracy or court promulgated. As de Tocqueville had also predicted, as America became more democratic, the people would lose interest in limiting government power, for they would see it as limiting themselves.[7]

While the change was gradual, beginning during the Civil War, Woodrow Wilson was the first prominent leader to directly challenge the division of powers itself. Major modifications were made by him as president and especially by his successor, Franklin Roosevelt, during the Great Depression. But the turning point may have been the 1960s-1970s counterculture unrest and the following political instability of the John Kennedy and Martin Luther King assassinations that resulted in breaking the remaining institutional powers centers independent of the national system—first, the urban Democratic political machines and the Southern Democratic Party by the welfare system, the civil rights revolution, and the democratization of the nomination and electoral systems; second, the decline in popular attachment to the mainline establishment Protestant denominations; third, the weakening of the family by welfare policies and ideologies that made single parenthood more economically sustainable; and, fourth, the replacement of local, main street media by three national television networks. Finally, this new media—later joined by cable competitors—broadcast a new morality of a "Me Generation" that distained individual moral obligations to community, religious, associational, and governmental institutions.

As a result, national government in the U.S. has lost a great degree of its moral authority, especially on domestic matters. Liberals cannot reform it because people will not trust its experts with greater power nor pay higher taxes for new programs or eliminate existing programs to free funds for new policy endeavors. Conservatives cannot summon the political will to redirect national power back to local and private alternatives. From both left and right there is the desire to rebuild a moral, responsible citizenry that will consider one's neighbor and community and even volunteer in their cause. But there is a cultural divide over whether this means a return to traditional values and active, local citizenship or a further liberalization of them and greater deference to national experts. It is beyond the means of this short book to settle these matters, and it is not the job of authors in any event as, ultimately, the people and their leaders will make their own decision.

Drift is one course and, perhaps, the most likely one given the ideological standoff. But this could end in the bankruptcy of the government from its massive Social Security and Medicare obligations. As the authoritative World Bank data make clear, Western ideas are relatively restricted in geographical reach and have not extended very deeply into world society. While democracy has spread, the more important rule of law and respect for property have not gained much international traction. As the looming crisis over entitlements for the elderly suggests, the United States itself is not immune from the temptations to defer unpopular decisions and rule by will rather than by law and override property rights to delay the day of reckoning. The Western experiment, especially the American version, has not lasted all that long by historical standards, and there is no guarantee that it will be maintained if the will and moral commitment that created it are not sustained.

NOTES

1. Genesis 1–2.

2. Aristotle, *Nichomachean Ethics*, trans. Davis Ross (London: Oxford University Press, 1925), I: 8.

4. J. C. Murray, "Medieval Synthesis," in *Death of God* (New Haven, Conn.: Yale University Press, 1942), 87–95.

5. Fareed Zakaria, *The Future of Freedom* (New York: Norton, 2003), 34.

6. John Emerich Edward Dalberg-Acton, *Essays in the Study and Writing of History* (Indianapolis: Liberty Classics, 1986), chap. 2.

7. Alexis de Tocqueville, *Democracy in America*, trans. Henry Reeve, (London: Saunders & Otley, 1840), II: 4, vi. Also see John Stewart Mill, *On Liberty* (New York: Norton, 1975), 1–5.

Index

About the Author

Donald Devine, the former director of the U.S. Office of Personnel Management, holds the Grewcock chair in American values at Bellevue University. He is a Washington Times columnist, a writer, an adjunct scholar at The Heritage Foundation, and a Washington policy consultant. He was President Reagan's head of Federal personnel from 1981–85 and had advised him previously beginning in 1976. He was a senior advisor to Bob Dole from 1988 to 1996 and to Steve Forbes between 1998–2000. For 14 years, Dr. Devine was associate professor of government and politics at the University of Maryland, specializing in democratic theory, public opinion and policy. Devine is the author of six books, the *Attentive Public*, *The Political Culture of the United States*, *Does Freedom Work?*, *Reagan Electionomics*, *Reagan's Terrible Swift Sword*, and *Restoring the Tenth Amendment*. He was senior editor of Western Vision and American Values, a book of readings on Western civilization for Bellevue University Press. He lives in Shadyside, Maryland, is married to Ann S. Devine and they have four children and eleven grandchildren.